PARTICULAR
DELIGHTS

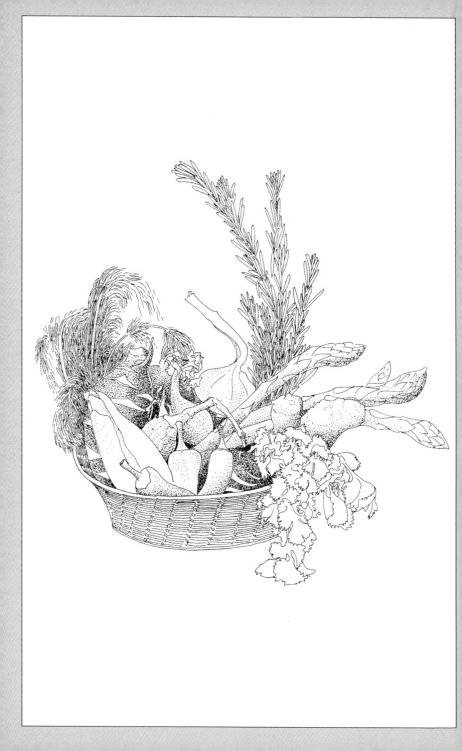

PARTICULAR DELIGHTS

COOKING FOR ALL THE SENSES

NATHALIE HAMBRO

Grub Street · London

Published in 2013 by
Grub Street
4 Rainham Close
London
SW11 1HT
Email:food@grubstreet.co.uk
Web: www.grubstreet.co.uk
Twitter: @grub_street

First published 1981 by Jill Norman & Hobhouse Ltd

A CIP record for this book is available from the British Library
ISBN 978-1-908117-39-7

Jacket design and formatting Sarah Driver

Printed and bound in India

CONTENTS

INTRODUCTION

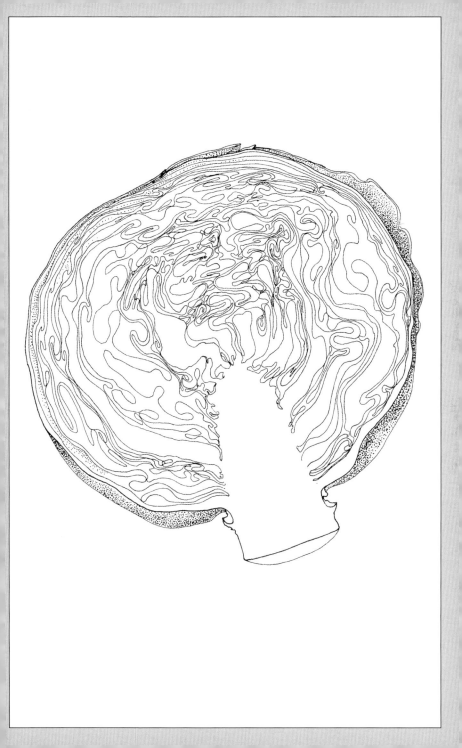

Cookery means the knowledge of Medea, and of Circe, and of Calypso, and of Helen, and of Rebekah, and of the Queen of Sheba. It means the knowledge of all herbs, and fruits, and balms, and spices; and of all that is healing and sweet in fields and groves, and savoury in meats; it means carefulness, and inventiveness, and watchfulness, and willingness, and readiness of appliance; it means the economy of your great-grandmothers, and the science of modern chemists; it means much tasting, and no wasting; it means English thoroughness, and French art, and Arabian hospitality; and it means, in fine, that everybody has something nice to eat.

John Ruskin, *The Ethics of the Dust.*
Ten lectures to little housewives

This book is about the art of eating, a rather wider notion than the art of cooking. Whereas cooking can be merely a mechanical execution of the instructions in a cookery book, eating involves the use of all the senses. Life can be enhanced by the sensual elements in our surroundings. Forgotten memories are evoked by smell throughout life, and what can compare with the everyday smells of freshly roasted coffee and of bread as it is baked, or the delicate ratafia scent of plum or cherry jam as it cooks?

The five physical senses are intimately connected. For example, taste is closely associated with smell and we need both these senses to savour food. When one has a cold, the tongue, without the support of the sense of smell, can scarcely relay the crudest information as to sweetness, sourness, saltiness, pungency. The tongue imparts to the brain a sort of magnified image of what is in the mouth, for tasting is tactile sensitivity as well as mere identification of flavour. The creamy smoothness of a plain avocado pear is entirely different from the smoothness of a guacamole, where the natural texture of the fruit has been destroyed. The texture of a sweet pear is something else again, harder and juicier, yet not as hard as that of the apple, whose grain feels closer; and in a grapefruit we notice the tiny juice capsules in each segment. When you are buying fruit, use the senses of smell and touch as well as that of sight. To choose a melon, gently press its top or bottom and smell the aroma which is released. Once your shopkeeper or stallholder knows that you select carefully from his range of fruits and vegetables, he will respect you and allow you to sample various produce if you are a regular customer. The French seem more conscious of quality and even the humblest stallholder displays his wares with aesthetic intuition. In Italy too, fruit is cut open for the customer to sample, so that he can appreciate the texture, colour and perfume before purchasing.

Gradually from childhood we build up an individual reference of textures, aromas and tastes, and this helps to ensure that the dishes we prepare complement one another; but we should not forget visual appeal. The appearance of a dish, while it may not affect the taste, will affect our anticipation. It might seem that hearing is the least important sense when it comes to eating, but in its subtle way it contributes to our enjoyment, giving us pleasure in the clink of the ice in a glass, the dull thud of a spoon as it strikes the side of a soufflé dish and the laughter surrounding the feast.

To discuss the senses one by one may seem an absurdity. Consciously or not, we are using them all at one and the same time, to evaluate, select or reject. But by becoming more aware of the use of the senses, we can not only learn but improve the quality of life about us. If we listen rather than hear, feel rather than touch, savour rather than taste, look rather than see, we are then left only with the sense of smell which is beyond our control, and perhaps it is not desirable that we should be able to curb this spontaneous sensibility.

When planning a meal, bear in mind that you need to use more than the physical senses. You will need to use your sense of balance to ensure that you create a harmony between the dishes you produce, for there will be something amiss otherwise, however good they are individually. There are, of course, many levels on which this equilibrium is needed – texture, colour, temperature, taste. Textures run from smooth to rough, from soft to crisp and crunchy, and you should serve a creamy dish followed by a crisp salad, for example. Look with a painter's eye at the colours of the dishes you decorate and present, to be sure that they satisfy the eye like a good still life. If a meal starts with a cold soup, try a hot pudding to finish, and vice versa. If one dish is spicy, accompany it with another which will refresh and clean the palate. Many of the recipes in this book combine sweet and sour and therefore have an intriguing combination of their own.

I like to have many small dishes, eaten together, rather than a set starter, main course and pudding. If the idea of cooking and washing up so many courses appals you, do not be alarmed. It is surprising how much can be prepared in advance, and changing plates for each course is not necessary at all if you plan things that fit well together.

There is no need to go to great extremes of fussiness, as did the Edwardians who dressed up dull dishes to look like sand-castles. The beauty of natural ingredients is that they speak for themselves. It requires no effort to present cheeses on a darkly curling cabbage leaf, or on fig or mulberry leaves. Use baskets for bread and toast, and clean linen, sparkling glasses and cutlery, candlelight, flowers and red wine glowing in the decanters. Each will contribute to the enjoyment of the simplest of meals as much as the food itself. It is important not to overdo things, but on special occasions it is rewarding to go a little further by serving ice cream on a block of coloured ice, or perhaps freezing summer flowers in clear ice and producing them as if by magic at a winter dinner table, surrounding a vodka bottle. Allow your imagination free rein. Put vanilla or rosemary into your sugar storage jar, drink scented teas, flavour your vinegar with herbs and fruits, steep fresh basil in oil, place bowls of pot-pourri about the house, or burn scented candles or juniper sticks.

Plan your wines well ahead of time, so that they will be in the right condition. It is thoughtful to offer an alternative to coffee after dinner, as so many people find it interferes with their sleep. Offer a jasmine tea, or a tisane (an infusion of lime or mint for example), which are not expensive.

One last point, which is no less important: when the first guest arrives, you should not worry about the food any more. After all, real friends care more about you than about the success of the meal.

The recipes in this book may be unusual, but on the whole they are simple and inexpensive to prepare. What makes them, to my mind, different and interesting is the unusual use of familiar ingredients to give a familiar dish a new flavour. I have experimented with various combinations, trying to be imaginative and adventurous. Any formality is quite unintentional in my way of cooking and eating; I prefer that culinary beauty should appear to be accidental, and that gentle music and amusing conversation add the finishing touch and create the mood around the table.

The recipes will serve six people unless otherwise stated.

CHEESE DISHES

I make some of my own soft cheeses and crème fraîche, and although I live in London this, together with preserving and bread-making, gives me the illusion of running something like a country kitchen. White cheese in a muslin-lined colander, the whey dripping into a brown glazed earthenware jug, is a very pleasant sight in the kitchen.

CRÈME FRAÎCHE

This is the homemade version of the French crème fraîche. Though similar in taste to English sour cream, it is much richer, with a higher fat content. It has the advantage of not curdling when boiled.

The following method makes a cream with a nutty, slightly sour taste. Yogurt gives a sourer tang than sour cream. The crème fraîche will keep up to a month in the refrigerator.

250 ml/½ pint double cream	250 ml/½ pint sour cream or yogurt

Put both creams (or cream and yogurt) in a saucepan and heat until just more than lukewarm. Pour into an earthenware or glass jar (which you have rinsed under hot water and dried in order to keep the cream at the same temperature). Cover with 2 tea-cloths to maintain a constant temperature. Leave overnight. The cream will have thickened. Stir, cover and refrigerate.

FROMAGE BLANC

After first nibbling a pink biscuit, Jean would crush his strawberries into a portion of cream cheese until the resultant colour gave promise of the taste long dreamed of and now, in a moment or two to become reality.

Meanwhile, he would add a few strawberries and a scrap more cream, in carefully calculated proportion, pleasure fighting with

concentration in his eyes, with all the accumulated experience of a
colourist and the intuition of an epicure.

Marcel Proust, *Jean Santeuil*

Fromage blanc is a soft cheese, which differs in taste and texture from cream cheese and curd cheese. It is costly to buy, but making your own is as simple as making yogurt. It has a fresh cheese taste and a fairly high moisture content, and for this reason is best eaten fresh.

Soft cheese is made by coagulating milk or cream, or both, then draining off some of the liquid (whey). The process takes 8 to 10 hours' incubation, except for the first time which requires 24 hours for the cheese to form, then about $1\frac{1}{2}$ to $2\frac{1}{2}$ hours for the draining, depending on what you intend to use it for.

I use fromage blanc as a pudding with crunchy sugar dredged over it, or with home-made jam, or as a savoury with chopped fresh herbs beaten in when ready. It makes marvellous cold sauces or dressings, added to fragrant walnut oil, or mixed with spices and added to cream, mayonnaise or yogurt.

The richness depends on the milk or cream used, and you can combine silver-top or gold-top milk, single, double or Jersey cream.

This is the way I suggest you make the first batch. I know the method looks complicated on paper, but it is quite simple in practice, and doesn't require any special equipment.

1–$1\frac{1}{2}$ litres/ 2–3 pints fresh milk
2 Petit-Suisse or Gervais cream
   cheeses, about 1 tablespoon

5–6 drops cheese rennet
(available from good grocers)

Use the milk of your choice (or partly substitute cream). For the first batch only, boil the milk, then cool to just above lukewarm (72°F/22°C). Warm a large bowl with boiling water, then dry thoroughly. (The warmed container will help maintain the right temperature during incubation.) With a fork or wire whisk, beat the tablespoon of fromage blanc (your starter) in the bowl, add the tepid milk gradually, beating all the time. Stir in the few drops of cheese rennet. Cover with a piece of cling-film and one large towel folded over.

The milk (and cream if used) will take about 24 hours to sour and coagulate the first time. When set, spoon out 5 tablespoons of the curds, placing each in a small, plastic, airtight container and freeze. This will be your starter for the next batches.

Line a sieve or colander with a cheesecloth or double thickness of muslin which you have dampened and wrung out, and suspend it over a bowl. Pour the remaining soft cheese into the lined colander or sieve, taking care to break the curd as little as possible. (One or two brisk shakes will detach the cheese from the sides, and with a little luck the whole block should slide off gently.) Leave in a cool place to allow some of the whey to drip out. How long you drain the cheese depends on how firm you wish to have the fromage blanc, but in any case it will take between 1½ and 2½ hours.

Scrape the cheese from the cloth into a bowl with a stainless steel or silver spoon (otherwise you may give the cheese a metallic taste). You should have lost about half of the initial volume. Reserve the whey for making cakes or bread, using it instead of buttermilk. Beat the fromage blanc until smooth with a fork or a small wire whisk. As a matter of taste, if eaten straight with sugar and jam, or seasoned with salt and pepper with potato and caraway bread (p. 41) I prefer the coarse texture, but for dressings, I beat it as prescribed. Cover and refrigerate for 1 hour before using, to let it get firm. It will keep for about 5 days, but it is at its best when really fresh.

Lastly it is very important to rinse and boil the cloth to sterilise it after each use.

When you have finished your last supply of the starter, you should repeat this process in order to make a new batch of high quality starter to freeze.

METHOD II
If you only have junket rennet available, follow this method instead, using the longer incubation (24 hours) each time, as the curd will take longer to set properly.

150 ml/¼ pint cream   1 ½ litres/3 pints milk
(single or double)   1 tablespoon junket rennet

Warm the milk and cream together. Stir in the rennet, turn into a bowl.
Cover and leave for up to 24 hours, depending on the temperature of
the room. Then proceed as for the previous recipe.

BARQUETTES DE FROMAGE

This is time-consuming, but fun to prepare. The little pieces of cream
cheese are presented on a bed of green leaves laid on a flat dish. The
array of colours given by the various spices and herbs makes it look
like a painter's palette. Though the same cheese is used as a base, the
different tastes and colours make it very versatile indeed. Everyone
samples tiny morsels of each cheese.

HERBS AND SPICES

paprika   cumin seeds
cayenne pepper   dried thyme
powdered cinnamon   powdered sage
coarse black pepper   curry powder
caraway seeds   turmeric

INGREDIENTS TO DECORATE THE TOP

raisins soaked in alcohol   pine nuts
currants   pumpkin seeds
walnut halves   split almonds
whole peppercorns   pistachio nuts

For this recipe I buy several wrapped cream cheeses which come in
a neat, squarish shape. Each one is cut into four. Each piece is then
rolled in the spice or herb of your choice and topped with one of the
decorative ingredients.

FONTAINEBLEAU CHEESE

In France, a pudding we loved as children was *Fontainebleau*, a kind of cream cheese, airy and white like dove down. This recipe is the nearest thing to what my memory recalls. The addition of milk makes the cream lighter and more like that found in France.

FOR 4 PEOPLE

250 ml/½ pint double cream	1 egg white at room
2 tablespoons milk	temperature
	1 tablespoon caster sugar

First chill for 10 minutes, in the ice compartment of a refrigerator, a bowl containing the cream, milk and beater. (The chilling allows the cream to be beaten for longer without turning into butter.)

Meanwhile in another bowl beat the egg white until stiff. Reserve. Whip the cream and milk in the chilled bowl until firm. Fold in the sugar and then the egg white.

Transfer the mixture to a muslin-lined cheese mould (about 500-ml/1-pint capacity) or 4 individual heart-shaped porcelain moulds with perforated bottoms. If you haven't any of these, use a sieve, but in any case the moulds should be muslin-lined. Leave to drain onto a plate or a tray for 6–8 hours in a cool place or a refrigerator.

Just before serving, turn out onto a dish, remove the muslin and bring to the table with more sugar and homemade tomato jam (p. 180), or in summer with red fruits.

GRILLED CHAVIGNOL ON TOAST

I like to be able to improvise a light but epicurean meal in no time and without fuss. This dish works well for such occasions. *Crottins de Chavignol* are small goat cheeses, not very strong, about the size of big plums. I preserve them in olive oil with a sprig of thyme or rosemary. They are beautiful to look at, magnified in a glass jar, steeped in the yellow liquid with the silhouetted herb. The little cheeses can be kept that way for weeks, ready for use; their taste will mellow with time. When they are finished the flavoured oil can be used with lentils, broccoli, rice or any vegetable of your choice.

PER PERSON

1 slice white French-type bread	freshly ground black pepper
1 Chavignol goat cheese	

Toast the bread on both sides. Put in an ovenproof dish, placing the cheese on top. Coarsely grind over the top some black pepper and grill for a few minutes until the skin is lightly brown. Inside the cheese will have softened to a creamy consistency, and the heat will have released more of the flavour. Serve at once with a frisée (curly endive) and walnut salad.

FROMAGE EN SURPRISE

In this recipe a whole cheese is concealed in a golden pastry crust. When cut, the pastry flakes over the partially melted cheese. I try to get a small Brie type for this dish. Failing that, I use 3 Camemberts, but they need more pastry. Bought puff pastry is fine for this recipe. Serve with scarlet salad (p. 121) and maybe curried melon (p. 149) to start with.

250 g/8 oz puff pastry or 500 g/1 lb if using 3 cheeses	about 3 tablespoons melted butter
1 Brie or 3 Camembert cheeses	

Pre-heat the oven to gas 7/425°F/220°C.

FOR A BRIE ABOUT 20 CM/8 INCHES IN DIAMETER

Roll out 2 circles of pastry about 25 cm/9 inches in diameter. Lay one on a baking tray, place the cheese in the centre, cover with the other circle and seal, pressing with a fork all around, making a crimped border. Brush with melted butter and bake for 20 minutes.

FOR 3 CAMEMBERTS ABOUT 10 CM/4 INCHES IN DIAMETER
Roll out 6 circles of pastry about 15 cm/5½ inches in diameter. (Trim the pastry with a bread plate as they are normally the right size.) Lay 3 of the circles on a baking tray, place a cheese in the centre of each one and cover with the remaining circles and seal, pressing with a fork all around, making a crimped border. Brush with melted butter and bake for 15–20 minutes.

DEVILS IN OVERCOATS

This is a variation on devils on horseback. Here the bacon and a cheese-filled prune are wrapped in several layers of paper-thin filo pastry. The best way to deal with the pastry is to work only one sheet at a time, leaving the rest with a damp cloth or a plastic bag over them, otherwise the sheets tend to dry out and become brittle. The parcels may be re-heated successfully the following day. If you plan to do so, do not refrigerate them as they would lose their crispness, but leave at room temperature.

The devils in overcoats are good served with smoked fish or with roasted pheasant.

100 g/3 oz Stilton cheese
1 heaped tablespoon fennel seeds
20 stoned prunes
20 rashers streaky bacon, very thinly sliced

10 sheets filo pastry (from Greek grocers)
125 g/4 oz unsalted butter, melted

Mash together the Stilton and fennel seeds and put a little of this filling inside each prune. Roll a slice of bacon around each prune and reserve.

Prepare two parcels at a time: take one sheet of pastry and lay it flat on a board and brush it lightly with melted butter. Cut the sheet lengthways into two strips. Fold each strip in two and brush it again with butter. Place a bacon-wrapped prune on a corner and fold the corner over to form a triangle. Continue folding the pastry in triangles down to the full length of the strip, to make one multilayered triangle. Prepare the remaining strip in the same manner. Repeat the operation until all the filo pastry and bacon and prune parcels are used, each time covering the reserved pastry to prevent it from drying.

Place the devils in overcoats on a greased oven tray and brush each one with more butter. Pre-heat the oven to gas 5/375°F/190°C and bake the parcels for 25–30 minutes or until they are golden.

COTTAGE CHEESE PANCAKES

Maslyanitsa, the carnival week before Lent, is the great season for blinis in Russia. They are eaten with a variety of smoked fish and caviar, smeared with melted butter and sour cream.

These pancakes are not unlike blinis. They can be served as a savoury or a sweet course. With a little more salt added to the batter, they are delicious at breakfast with crispy bacon, or they may be served as a pudding with crunchy sugar or jam and sour cream.

Cottage cheese pancakes should be crisp outside, with a soft and creamy centre. I prefer to make them at the last minute, for they are at their best eaten as soon as they are done, but if they are to be made ahead of time, pile the pancakes on a plate, cover tightly with foil so they remain moist, and keep warm in the oven.

250 g/8 oz cottage cheese
2 eggs, lightly beaten
2 tablespoons flour
2 tablespoons melted butter
a pinch of salt

Mix all the ingredients together, and make sure no lumps remain. Leave to rest for at least an hour to allow the flour to swell. Heat a griddle or cast-iron omelette pan (don't grease it) and proceed as for normal pancakes, but make them thicker and about 8 cm/3 inches in diameter. In fact several can be made at the same time. Brown on both sides and serve.

PARMESAN PUFFS

These puffs will melt in the mouth. They should be eaten immediately, and for the best results I recommend using an electric deep-fryer, because the thermostat will ensure that the oil is kept at a constant temperature. The puffs go well with poultry or game as a side dish.

3 egg whites	nutmeg
150 g/5 oz grated Parmesan cheese	cayenne pepper
	fine breadcrumbs

Heat the deep-fryer set to its lowest temperature. Beat the egg whites until firm. Season the Parmesan with a little grated nutmeg and cayenne pepper. Gently fold the cheese into the egg whites. With a soup spoon, scoop out the mixture, rolling each scoop in the dry breadcrumbs. This operation is easier if you use a second, smaller spoon as well. Fry the puffs for a few minutes until golden. Drain on kitchen paper and serve at once.

EGG
DISHES

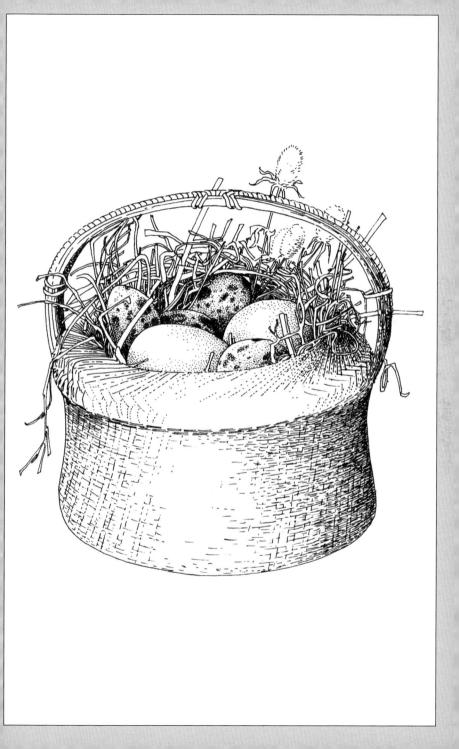

LAZY EGGS

This recipe is my husband's. A calorie-filled concoction to which it is easy to get addicted. The only 3 set ingredients are the eggs, the butter and the mayonnaise. The way of cooking them remains the same whatever other goodies you use. The idea is to use whatever is appetising in the refrigerator: some cream cheese, left-over cold potatoes, mushrooms or chopped broccoli. The herb you choose depends on what you are adding it to, and in general it is best to use only one. Mostly I use thyme, remembering to crush the little leaves in the palm of my hand before adding them, so that the aromatic oil is released from the leaf cells.

This is emphatically not a dinner party dish, because it is difficult to get it all ready at once in large quantities. I suggest it just for two (or even one if you are feeling greedy). You need some wholemeal bread for toasting, and a little bowl that will fit inside a saucepan for boiling eggs. Best of all, serve it with a crisp green salad, which must be ready before you start.

3 large eggs	a good knob of butter
1 tablespoon mayonnaise	salt
(bought will do very well)	freshly ground pepper

AS WELL AS THESE BASIC INGREDIENTS, USE AT LEAST
ONE OF THE FOLLOWING (OR SOMETHING SIMILAR)
AND THE SUGGESTED HERB OR SPICE

fresh cream cheese or Philadelphia	thyme
some little cold boiled potatoes, sliced	chives
some sweet corn kernels	dill weed
chopped ham, or crispy bacon (wonderful)	thyme
cold broccoli or a Brussels sprout or two	nutmeg
half a tomato, sliced	oregano
two or three sliced mushrooms	thyme

It is important to follow the sequence so as to get the hot eggs and toast to the table efficiently.

1 Put some cold water and salt in the egg pan and put it on the heat.

2 Get out your little bowl and put in it the knob of butter, the mayonnaise, the optional extra you have chosen, the herb, pepper and salt.

3 The water should be boiling by now; put in the eggs, and time for $4\frac{1}{2}$ minutes.

4 While they are cooking, cut the bread and put in the toaster, get out the toast rack.

5 The eggs should be done now. Take them out with a spoon, but do not throw out the hot water. Instead, place the bowl with the ingredients in the pan (off the fire or on very low heat) so they begin to warm up. (You may need to throw out a little water to be sure it doesn't spill into the bowl.)

6 Peel the eggs (which should be soft-boiled) partly under the cold tap, as quickly as you can without burning your fingers. As you finish each one, pop it into the bowl in which the butter should now be melted.

7 Mash the eggs and other ingredients and taste to ensure the seasoning is right. If the eggs are a little too cooked you could add a teaspoon of walnut oil. A couple of drops of sesame oil add an interesting flavour.

8 Take the bowl from the hot water. Dry it, and take it to the table with the toast. Eat with a teaspoon.

OEUFS POLONAIS

These eggs are traditionally served in Poland on Christmas Eve. The celebratory meal takes place early in the evening, after the first star is seen in the winter sky. I bring them to the table in a very shallow basket or on a wicker tray, with a little bundle of small horn spoons to scoop them out of their shells. They are so delicious and look so pretty that they deserve to be made more than once a year!

6 hard-boiled eggs	chopped
100 g/3 oz butter	salt
2–3 tablespoons parsley, finely	freshly ground pepper

With a very sharp kitchen knife, halve the eggs lengthwise, shell and all. Don't worry if little bits of the shell break, or the edges are uneven; in the end it won't show.

Scoop the whites and yolks out carefully into a bowl and chop, but do not mash them. Reserve the half shells. Melt 60 g/2 oz of the butter and pour over the eggs, mixing with a large fork. Add the finely chopped parsley, season to taste with the salt and the freshly ground pepper. With a small spoon refill the half shells, pressing lightly but firmly, leaving the egg mixture slightly heaped. The preparation up to this point can be done well in advance.

Just before serving, melt the remaining butter in a sauté pan. When it starts foaming, put in the eggs, open side down. Cook just for a few minutes, or until golden. Transfer with a large spoon (it is easier) onto a small wicker tray, brown side up.

OEUFS AU NID

This starter is made in a matter of minutes. It is a variation on *oeufs en cocotte*, but here the ramekin is replaced by an individual brown bread roll, which is eaten with the egg. The bread crust is crisp outside and flavoured with mace inside. Serve green meadow sauce (p.135) with it.

PER PERSON

1 small round wholemeal bread	1 egg
roll (one day old preferably)	powdered mace
a little butter	salt and freshly ground pepper

Set the oven to gas 4/350°F/180°C. Cut a hat from the roll and keep aside. Scoop out the inside, being careful not to break the crust, to leave a cavity big enough for the egg. (The breadcrumbs may be used for the brown bread praline recipe, p. 46.) Spread the bread shell with a little butter. Season. Break the egg into it. Sprinkle with mace, salt and pepper, and put on the middle shelf of the pre-heated oven for 8–10 minutes. The egg is ready when the white is opaque and no longer transparent. When it is ready, put the reserved hat back on and serve with the sauce.

VARIATION

Omit the green meadow sauce, and instead put a little piece of pâté or a few chopped raw mushrooms at the bottom of each roll, break in the egg and top it with a tablespoon of cream. Bake as for the above recipe.

⌒〰⌒

SUN ON A CLOUD

I like to make this recipe, which is easy although it looks very unusual. As you take the first mouthful, the yolk bursts in a dense orange stream over the feathery light cushions of the beaten egg white. Served with Balkan sauce (p. 136).

PER PERSON

1 egg	pinch of salt
2 tablespoons grated cheese	dusting of paprika
(Emmenthal or Gruyère)	½ large tomato, peeled

Pre-heat the oven to gas 7/425°F/220°C. Separate yolk and white. Put the latter in a mixing bowl with the salt and whisk until very firm. Fold the grated cheese in gently.

Have ready an oven tray lined with greased foil. Place on it the half tomato, cut side up. Make a little nest with the egg white on the tomato. Slide the egg yolk into the centre of the nest. Bake in the pre-heated oven for 3 minutes. Dust with paprika and serve at once.

⌒〰⌒

RAINBOW OMELETTE

For a summer lunch I like a simple herb omelette, chilled and sliced, served with a vinaigrette. Every so often it is worth taking the time to make this recipe which shows its glory when cut, and its coloured layers are revealed. It is a meal in itself, served with a green salad, and would be ideal for a picnic. The rainbow omelette may be prepared as early as 12 hours in advance, and it will serve 10–12 people.

FOR THE RED OMELETTES

8 eggs	a little thyme
4 tablespoons tomato paste	salt and white pepper
(Italian is best)	1 tablespoon cold water

Beat the eggs thoroughly with the tomato paste, thyme, salt and pepper. Lastly add the cold water (this is to lighten the mixture). In your omelette pan, fry 6 very thin omelettes, rather like pancakes, without turning them over. Reserve.

FOR THE GREEN OMELETTES

8 eggs	stalks as well)
2–3 bunches of watercress	salt and pepper
(chopped fine with some of the	1 tablespoon cold water

Beat the eggs thoroughly with the chopped watercress, salt and pepper; adding the cold water last. In your omelette pan, fry 6 very thin omelettes as above. Reserve.

FOR THE YELLOW LAYERS

60 g/2 oz butter	Cheddar or fontina
60 g/2 oz flour	salt
250 ml/½ pint milk	cayenne pepper
125 g/4 oz grated farmhouse	

Make a cheese sauce in the usual way, but rather on the thick side. Let it cool to lukewarm.

FOR THE PINK LAYERS

4 slices of ham, cut very thin   a little Dijon mustard

TO ASSEMBLE

When the omelettes are cooled, on a large piece of foil put a watercress omelette, cooked side down, spread it rather sparingly with some of the cheese sauce. Place a tomato omelette on top, cooked side up. Next put a slice of ham, spread lightly on both sides with a little mustard to make it sticky. Continue with alternate layers until all the omelettes, sauce and ham are used up. Wrap the rainbow-coloured pile in the foil carefully, press gently and chill overnight.

Just before serving, unwrap and cut in wedges, like a cake.

TARTE AUX OEUFS

This dish never fails to be a great success. The combination of flavours is a very happy one and the guests always wonder about the shell and the three-coloured wedges.

It is quite a substantial dish, which I serve as a main course. It should be balanced by something with a crunchy texture and a sharp taste. A side salad like the carrot and orange one (p. 127), or just a plain watercress salad, would be perfectly adequate.

Though the process seems lengthy, the tarte can be made step by step, and prepared 1 or 2 days ahead. The method is easy; the only tricky part is removing the shell from the flan tin, but it can be done if you leave the shell in the refrigerator long enough for it to become firm.

10 hard-boiled eggs
100 g/3 oz melted butter
½ packet gelatine dissolved in 2 tablespoons of cold water
150 ml/¼ pint homemade mayonnaise, fairly sharp

150 ml/¼ pint yogurt or sour cream (or a mixture of both)
125 g/4 oz left-over fresh salmon, flaked
freshly ground pepper
fresh chives

1 In a big bowl, chop the eggs evenly and fairly fine. Pour over the melted butter and mix lightly, using a fork to avoid mashing the eggs. No salt is necessary as the butter and the salmon are both slightly salted, but pepper generously. Line a 25-cm/10-inch flan dish with foil, or even better, use a flan ring, in which case you do not need to use foil, but can build the shell directly on the serving dish. Press down the egg mixture, flattening it with the back of a spoon. Raise the sides as you would do for short pastry. Chill in the refrigerator for at least 1 hour.

2 Meanwhile in a saucepan have 5 cm/2 inches of boiling water, off the fire. Set in it a bowl with the gelatine and the water, and leave until clear and smooth. Remove from the bain-marie.

3 Put the mayonnaise and the yogurt or sour cream, into another bowl or cup and lower into the saucepan of hot water. Leave until runny. Gradually blend in the gelatine and keep in the pan of hot water until needed. Make sure the water does not go cold; re-heat as necessary.

4 Take the well chilled egg shell out of the refrigerator. If you are using a flan dish, carefully lift the foil and transfer to the serving dish. If you are using a flan ring, run a knife around the shell to loosen it and remove the ring. Spread the flaked fish evenly on the top. Pour over the sauce, and chill for several hours, or even better, overnight.

5 Just before serving, peel off the foil. Decorate with a trellis pattern made with blades of fresh chive.

RED, GREEN AND YELLOW SCRAMBLE

This dish has 3 of the primary colours and a blend of tastes which are complementary. Serve with a salad with identical colours but contrasting textures made with beetroot, baby corn and lamb's lettuce. Good with savoury corn bread (p. 40).

8 large eggs	400 g tin red kidney beans
salt	2 tablespoons butter
freshly ground pepper	1 handful chopped parsley
Tabasco	

In a bowl, lightly beat the eggs and season with salt, pepper and 2–3 drops of Tabasco. Add the kidney beans, drained of liquid. Melt the butter in a heavy, preferably enamelled, pan, and cook until it begins to turn brown (*noisette*). Add the parsley and cook for a minute or two. Now pour in the eggs and swirl around with a wooden spatula to stop them sticking. The scrambled eggs are ready when they are just setting and still creamy. Serve at once as they go on cooking in the pan, even off the heat.

GRAIN, SEEDS AND NUTS

BREAD

The entire practical life and delight of a 'lady' is to be 'loaf-giver'
John Ruskin, *Fors Clavigera.*
Letters to the workmen and labourers of Great Britain

I know that many books have been written on the subject of bread, and I will not pretend to compete with them. All I should like to do is remove some of the mystery from baking by explaining how to gain confidence, and how to achieve success, even if it is partial at your first attempt.

First of all, bread-making is not a messy process if you work with a small quantity of flour, say 500 g/1 lb. (No mammoth batches of dough rising stickily to invade your kitchen like something out of a horror movie!) This amount will yield two small loaves. Seeds, herbs or grains can be added, or different flours can be mixed. My preferred blend is half wholemeal, half unbleached white. There is no need to panic about leaving the dough to rise. If you put it in a large plastic bag, which will protect it from draughts, the process will take between 2 and 4 hours if the dough is at room temperature. After the punching down and kneading, the second rising time is again flexible – it can even be omitted if you are in a hurry. In any case, dough has a will of its own and you will never receive a carbon-copy reaction, even were you to follow the directions minutely every time. This doesn't matter because whether your dough is chewy or light, dark or pale, it will always make good bread.

Another point which often puts people off baking their own bread is the time required for proving. As soon as they hear that a rising time of 2 or 4 hours is necessary, they sigh and claim that they haven't time to be doing this sort of thing. What they forget is that they are at liberty to go for a walk, or do the housework or see a movie. The bread doesn't care. It can look after itself without constant nursing.

The smell of baking bread is so earthy and wholesome, and the whole process so rewarding that once you have experimented you will keep on making it for your friends and family, even if you don't allow yourself to eat much of it.

Your own bread will be very much better than any from the so-called French bakeries in England. Indeed, I now find much of the bread in France tasteless or disappointing in texture, though Poilane in Paris still makes the most heavenly bread in the old-fashioned way, in wood-fired ovens. My favourites are their rye rolls and flaky apple *chaussons*.

WHOLEMEAL AND SESAME BREAD

This recipe makes a moist, nutty bread. The oatmeal or cracked wheat gives an earthy and chewy loaf. I find that sesame seeds bring a bacon-like flavour to the bread, particularly when toasted. For a richer bread, part or all of the water may be replaced by buttermilk. This bread keeps well even though only one rising is allowed.

15 g/½ oz fresh yeast or 2 teaspoons dried active yeast	1 tablespoon malt extract or molasses
4 tablespoons tepid water	350 g/¾ lb wholemeal flour
a pinch of sugar	125 g/4 oz strong white flour
generous 250 ml/½ pint warm water	250 g/8 oz coarse oatmeal or cracked wheat
2 teaspoons sea salt	3 tablespoons sesame seeds

Crumble or sprinkle the yeast into the tepid water, add the pinch of sugar and stir to dissolve. Leave to bubble and become frothy (about 10 minutes). In a jug, put the warm water, stir in the salt and malt extract or molasses. Reserve.

Mix together in a bowl the two flours, oatmeal or cracked wheat and sesame seeds. Add the yeast mixture to the salted warm water and pour gradually over the dry ingredients, incorporating roughly with a wooden spoon. When the dough gets too stiff and sticky to work, turn it onto a board sprinkled with more wholemeal flour and knead for 15 minutes or until the dough is smooth and pliable. Shape into a ball, pat it all over with oil and place in a large, greased bread tin, filling it about three quarters full. Cover and set in a warm place and leave to rise until doubled in bulk (it could take up to 4 hours if left at room temperature).

Pre-heat the oven for about 10 minutes to gas 4/350°F/180°C and bake the bread for 45 minutes. The loaf should sound hollow when removed from the tin and tapped on the bottom. Leave to cool on a rack.

SAVOURY CORN BREAD

This bread is a yellowish colour and the corn meal gives an unusual taste which goes well with the cheese and thyme. It can be sliced very thinly so it is suitable for toasting or sandwiches. This bread is good eaten with plenty of salted butter and black olives.

300 g/10 oz strong white flour
200 g/6 oz fine corn meal
1 tablespoon thyme
1 tablespoon dried yeast
dissolved in 3 tablespoons tepid water

1 tablespoon brown sugar
250 ml/½ pint warm water
2 teaspoons sea salt
100 g/3 oz grated Cheddar cheese

Mix the first 3 ingredients thoroughly in a crock or large bowl. Add the sugar to the yeast and tepid water, leave to stand for 10–15 minutes or until frothy. Dissolve the salt in the warm water.

Add the foaming yeast to the dry ingredients, mix in roughly with a wooden spoon, then little by little add the salted water, stirring the flour mixture into the centre of the bowl. With floured hands, knead just enough to make a compact ball. Cover with a cellophane paper or a damp and then a dry cloth, taking care to protect the dough from draught. Leave to rise for about 3½ hours in an airing cupboard or cold oven.

Meanwhile, brush two 500-g/1-lb bread tins with oil. When the dough has doubled in bulk (about 3 hours) punch it down with your fist. Sprinkle some extra corn meal and the grated cheese around the bowl and start kneading: fold in two, push down with your palms, turn the dough half a turn, fold in two etc., getting up a proper rhythm. Flour lightly when the dough starts to become sticky. After the first 6 turns you will have incorporated all the cheese. Continue kneading for 7–10 minutes, or until the dough feels elastic. Divide the ball in two and shape each half to fit its tin. It should come three quarters of the way up the sides. Then take the dough out and put it back in the tin upside down so that it is oiled on all sides. Cover properly and leave to rise again for about 3 hours, or until the dough reaches the top of the tins.

Pre-heat the oven for 10 minutes to gas 7/425°F/220°C, with a fireproof bowl or pan filled with water on the bottom shelf. (This will create steam in the oven and should be left in until the end of baking.)

At the end of the second rising, put both tins on the centre shelf of the oven and bake for 20 minutes. Then turn the oven down to gas 5/375°F/190°C for 25 minutes. Take the loaves out of the tins, loosening the sides with a knife (the cheese might stick) and leave to cool on a rack for about 2 hours.

The bread will keep in a plastic bag or a bread bin for up to 10 days. If you want to freeze it, keep it for 3 days before slicing and freezing, as I find that if I slice and freeze very fresh bread the slices tend to stick together because of their high moisture content.

POTATO AND CARAWAY BREAD

This recipe makes a light bread with a refreshing taste of caraway seeds. When toasted, the flavour of the potato is more pronounced. I use this bread for toasted sandwiches, but when doing so, leave the cut slices to dry out for 1 or 2 hours at room temperature. The potato should still be hot when you rice it as this makes it easier to mix with the flour.

FOR 2 SMALL LOAVES

1 teaspoon dried yeast
2 tablespoons warm water
1 heaped tablespoon coarse salt
250 ml/½ pint buttermilk or milk, warmed

125–175 g/4–6 oz floury potato, cooked unpeeled and still hot
500 g/1 lb strong flour
1 level tablespoon caraway seeds

Stir the yeast in the warm water and leave for 10 minutes or until frothy. Add the salt to the buttermilk or milk and stir until dissolved. Peel the hot potato and rice it over the flour through a coarse sieve. Blend it in with a fork until it resembles coarse meal. Sprinkle over the caraway seeds and then add the yeast mixture and buttermilk or milk. Knead for a minute or two. Leave the dough to rise, covered with a polythene bag, until doubled in bulk, about 2–3 hours.

With your fist, punch down the dough to release the air and reduce it to its initial volume. Knead for 7–10 minutes. Grease 2 small bread tins. Divide the dough in 2 and put it in the tins. Invert and replace the dough upside down in the tins, so that the greased bottoms are on top. Cover with the polythene bag and leave to rise a second time for 2–3 hours.

Pre-heat the oven to gas 6/400°F/200°C for 10 minutes with a metal tray filled with water placed on the bottom shelf, (the steam will give the bread a crisper crust). Bake for 45 minutes. Remove the loaves from the tins and leave them to cool upside down on a rack.

BANANA BREAD

This bread, though sweet, is good eaten during a meal as it makes a pleasant contrast to spicy dishes. It adds a delicate touch served as warm toast with a chilled soup. In the southern states of America it is part of a traditional Sunday brunch. Banana bread is delicious too at tea time with créole jam (p. 184) or coconut and lemon curd (p. 184).

125 g/4 oz wholemeal flour	a little yogurt or milk
125 g/4 oz unbleached flour	60 g/2 oz butter
3 teaspoons baking powder	60 g/2 oz dark brown sugar
a pinch of salt	grated rind of lemon
3 large ripe bananas	1 large egg

Pre-heat the oven to gas 5/375°F/190°C. Sift together the wholemeal flour, unbleached flour, baking powder and salt. Mash the bananas and combine with the yogurt or milk, stirring just enough to mix.

Cream butter and sugar together until very light. Add the lemon rind and beat in the egg. Add the dry ingredients alternately with the banana mixture, stirring just enough to combine well.

Turn into an oiled 23 x 13-cm/9 x 5-inch bread tin. Bake for 50–55 minutes or until done. Cool in the tin for 10 minutes, then remove and finish cooling on a rack.

BURGHUL AND YOGURT SALAD

Burghul is the roasted cracked wheat used mainly in Middle Eastern cooking. I am so fond of *tabbouleh* (a delicious, refreshing salad made with burghul, lemon, parsley and mint) that I thought up another salad using the same grain. In my recipe, the burghul is soaked for about 4 hours in yogurt. As I make my own yogurt regularly, I sometimes have a batch that will not be fresh by the time I return after a week-end away, so I prepare this salad which uses up a great quantity of yogurt. The addition of cumin gives a definite Middle Eastern flavour.

In France, every North African grocer stocks three sizes of burghul. (They call it bulgur, but the spelling varies.) Here you will find it in Greek grocers' or health food shops. I prefer to use the coarser sort for this salad, but if you choose one of the finer kinds the soaking time will be reduced to about a third.

If you have some salad left over, it can make a filling for tomatoes or aubergines. Or even better, for a quickly made starter, take a mixture of red, yellow and green peppers, cut a 'hat' from the stalk end, discard all the seeds and fill them with the burghul salad. Serve the stuffed peppers upright, with their hats on. They make a colourful dish.

600 ml/1 pint homemade yogurt, or a little more
175 g/6 oz burghul
1 teaspoon ground cumin

20 leaves of fresh mint, shredded with scissors
salt and freshly ground pepper

Put the yogurt in a large bowl. Stir in the burghul, cumin and shredded mint leaves. Season with salt and freshly ground pepper. Leave to soak, covered with a plate, for about 4 hours, stirring from time to time. The mixture which is quite runny at the beginning sets as the cracked wheat expands. The swollen grains should have a soft outside and be a little firm in the centre. Check for seasoning and refrigerate until needed. The salad will keep for a day or two in the refrigerator.

CREAM OF SESAME

This was inspired by Middle Eastern recipes, but it is a lighter dish as water and lemon, rather than oil, are used to achieve the right consistency. The oil is included for its taste, and only to emphasise the sesame flavour. As for the purple garlic, it is less pungent than the white English kind and it stays fresh longer. It is useful to know that if you split an old garlic clove in two lengthways and remove the little green shoot embedded in the centre, it makes it much easier to digest.

Serve with pitta bread toasted on both sides and cut in two. The pouches thus made can be filled with a few lettuce leaves and the cream of sesame.

175 g/6 oz whole sesame seeds
1 tablespoon sesame oil
few shavings of purple garlic
juice of 1 lemon
salt and pepper

pinch of cumin powder
1 teaspoon honey
water as necessary (or a mixture of yogurt and water)

Sieve the sesame seeds, as they tend to have a little grit left in them, and then grind them in batches in your coffee grinder (which you should first clean by grinding in it a torn slice of bread). In a bowl add the ingredients in the order listed and mix well. The water must be added gradually until the required consistency is reached. I like it supple but not runny.

MOORISH OATS

A quickly made treat when you are hungry. Moorish oats are wonderful as a filling for avocados, or as an accompaniment for lazy eggs (p. 28). This is a good way to use walnut oil, as there is nothing to distract from its nutty taste. Turmeric has a nearly indiscernible taste, but is used here to give colour.

The name Moorish is a play on words as people tend to ask for more!

PER PERSON

6 heaped tablespoons rolled oats	a pinch of turmeric
2–3 tablespoons walnut oil	celery salt
	freshly ground black pepper

In a small bowl, blend together thoroughly all the dry ingredients. Coat with the oil and eat without delay.

GRANOLA

Granola is an American breakfast cereal and is normally sold at health food shops for a high price. This homemade version is superior and more economical. I think that granola has a better texture than muesli and stays crisp even with milk or yogurt poured over it. The nuts should be left with the skin on. Don't try to chop them evenly: it is nice to find different sized pieces in the mixture.

Granola makes a delicious snack to nibble for lunch, or can be used as a base for the date and oat slices (p. 173).

3 cups rolled oats	½ cup sesame seeds (optional)
1 cup bran flakes	½ cup sunflower oil
1 cup desiccated coconut	½ cup honey
1 cup hazelnuts or almonds, chopped	1 teaspoon pure vanilla extract
½ cup wheat germ (optional)	1 cup large muscat raisins

Pre-heat the oven to gas 4/350°F/180°C. In a large crock, put the rolled oats, bran flakes, coconut, nuts, wheat germ and sesame seeds. In a small, heavy saucepan heat the oil and honey, stirring with a wooden spoon. When the honey is runny and partly blended with the oil, take off the heat, add the vanilla extract, and pour over the granola mixture. Toss very thoroughly, lifting the cereals from underneath to ensure even coating.

Spread the mixture on an oven tray and bake for 25–30 minutes. Stir with a spoon from time to time, checking that the sides and top are not getting too brown. Be more careful during the last 10 minutes of baking. The granola is ready when an even golden brown. When it is ready, put back in the crock and add the raisins. Leave to cool. By then it will have become crunchy.

Store in a large, old-fashioned, earthenware jar with a tight lid or cork. Granola will keep for months in a dry, cool place.

<hr/>

BROWN BREAD PRALINE

As I dislike wasting any food, here is a recipe to use up the wholemeal breadcrumbs left over from the recipe for *oeufs au nid* (p. 30). The result is a crunchy praline-like mixture which can be added to vanilla ice-cream (the praline is incorporated when the cream is half frozen), or used as a topping for custard-based puddings or baked fruits like apples or apricots.

100 g/3 oz stale wholemeal bread	100 g/3 oz sugar
60 g/2 oz unsalted butter	1 teaspoon cinnamon or allspice

Crumble the bread, not too finely, and fry it in the butter until crisp. Sprinkle on the sugar and spice and allow it to caramelise to a pale golden colour. Transfer the mixture to a wooden board and leave to cool.

YELLOW PANCAKES WITH COCONUT SAUCE

Chick-pea flour is normally used in Indian cooking for thickening soups and sauces. But one day when I was short of white flour I took a chance and added chick-pea flour to a batter. The result was feather-light pancakes, very easy to swirl around the pan, which came out paper-thin, and had a delicate flavour. They freeze so well that I like to make a large stack of them. For an impromptu meal, all you have to do is make the filling and the sauce, which both take very little time. Serve with spectrum salad (p. 119).

BATTER FOR 24 PANCAKES

60 g/2 oz white flour	250 ml/½ pint milk
60 g/2 oz chick-pea (gram) flour	salt
2 large eggs	

SAUCE

250 ml/½ pint single cream	soy sauce
60 g/2 oz desiccated coconut	salt and cayenne pepper

FILLING

500 g/1 lb spring greens	root
1 tablespoon oil	60 g/2 oz desiccated coconut
300 g/10 oz ricotta cheese	1 tablespoon soy sauce
125 g/4 oz toasted walnuts	salt and pepper
4-cm/1½-inch piece fresh ginger	butter

Make the batter in the usual way, ensuring that no lumps are left, sieving the mixture if necessary. Leave for about 1 hour to allow the flour to swell. I use two 15-cm/6-inch frying pans for making the pancakes. Brush the pans with a little oil or butter between pancakes. Working simultaneously with the two pans, stack the pancakes on a plate, brown side down, covering the pile with foil or greaseproof paper to keep them moist.

Trim the end of the hard stems from the spring greens. Clean, dry and chop into 2-cm/½-inch pieces. In a sauté pan heat the oil, put in the vegetables, then raising the heat to the maximum toss constantly with a wooden spatula until the greens are reduced by half. They should be slightly browned outside, but still crunchy. (This should take about 6–7 minutes.)

In a bowl, mash the ricotta with a fork. Add the walnuts, coarsely chopped. Peel and shred the ginger root very finely; add to the cheese mixture. Beat in the coconut and the soy sauce. Check and adjust the seasoning. Lastly incorporate the spring greens.

Grease generously an ovenproof dish large enough to hold the pancakes. Roll them around a little of the filling and lay on the dish, seam side down. Dot the tops with a little butter. Cover tightly with foil. (Up to this stage the recipe can be prepared ahead of time.) Heat in a moderate oven for about 30 minutes.

Make the sauce at the last minute. Warm the cream over a gentle heat. Stir in the desiccated coconut and the soy sauce. Season with salt and cayenne pepper (the sauce should be quite spicy). Pour the sauce over the pancakes as the dish is brought to the table. Sprinkle with more cayenne.

FISH

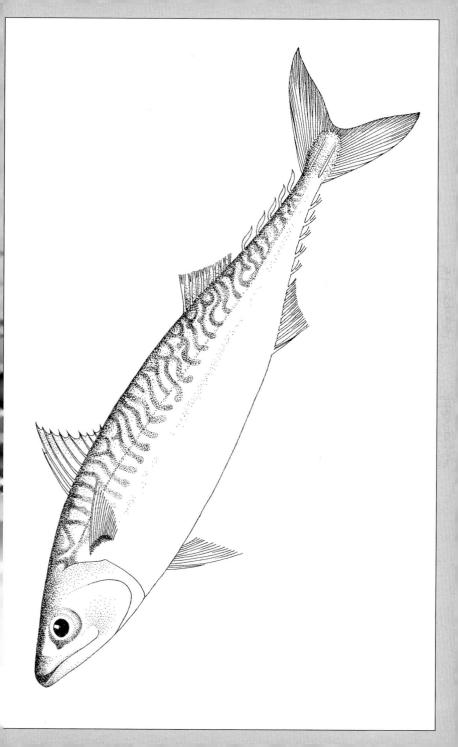

O Life was jolly in the sunlight, splashing the cod around. Water playing on our slab, ferns as cool as green, the whitest tiles in town.

It was my happy job to set the fish for show. I'd take a turbot say for central, a heavy fellow white and round. Then red lobsters, I'd ring my lobsters round that turbot, all their noses in, to make the petals of a flower. Then I'd take a cut of haddock, place this yellow by the turbot's head. I don't know why I put that haddock at the head, more than at the tail or sides. I don't know what I did not half the time. But it always came out right. I've that eye for colour: and I'd parsley my lobsters, green to red.

Now I had my white coat and my blue apron, now I'd jam my straw on pleased to greet the trade. But first I could finish off – now I'd got my central. Mackerel, trouts and my red spotted plaicelings – those coloured fellows I'd take next. Striped mackerels I'd make into a ring and place a crab within. Two rings I'd make, one each side to balance. Then stars of rainbow trout, all wet colours of the rainbow dew. But my plaice – my good brown plaice with the bright red dabs, these I'd bend tail to head, tail to head so they'd make a round, and I'd set them plumb in middle below the big turbot, for a braver marked fish would be hard to find.

And right down further – though this was not the least important – there'd be ordinaries . . . the herrings, the whiting, the cod. They'd go on trays. But I'd range them neatly as the rest: and in their middle place a tray of rich pink shrimps. But my long fish, you'll say? My three H's, rule of three and thumb, haddock and hake and halibut? My pike if you like? Yes, they'd all come in – they'd come in squaring up the rest, they'd come for squaring up. I'd put a lemon in a big pike's mouth, lemon to teeth, and sometimes there'd be mullet like coral and bream as pink as brown babies. And soles with their faces all one side – a tearful sight.

Scallops? What with my scallops? Lump them in the middle, a bunch of fresh-poached eggs? Make circles of them round my soles? Line them up to write my name? Not I! That I never would! . . . . No, I'd put one of them here and one of them there, and more of them there and another here – so they'd be eyed all over the place. And if Jim-at-the-back came front and queried, 'Where's your poached, my Charley-boy, my Barley?' – I'd wink and tell him: 'Look for yourself, Jim.' And he'd look, you know, he'd look for such a while before he'd see them! But after, he'd see them everywhere, he'd see nothing but these scallops. 'You could knock me down,' Jim'd say. I'd say, 'That's art, Jim.'

William Sansom, Lord Love Us (Hogarth Press, 1954)

CEVICHE

Ceviche is a South American dish of marinated fish. Only the freshest fish should be used for this, as the only cooking is provided by the lime juice. In ceviche the sea flavour is strongly developed and yet subtle. For the dressing, the olive oil can be replaced by fromage blanc (p. 16).

about 500 g/1 lb Dover sole, lemon sale or plaice fillets	1 teaspoon fennel seeds
6 limes or 4 lemons	10 green peppercorns
150 ml/¼ pint fruity olive oil	sea salt
3 blades giant chives or 2–3 spring onions	freshly ground black pepper

Cut the fish in thin diagonal strips. Squeeze the juice from the limes or lemons, cover the fish with it and refrigerate for 4 hours or so. Drain well. Combine the oil, chopped chives or spring onions (reserving some of the green), fennel seeds, green peppercorns, and pour over the fish strips. Season to taste, tossing lightly. Garnish, snipping over the reserved chives or green part of the spring onion.

MUSSEL SALAD

I love the little fish barrows of London street markets, the vendors with their friendly chatter, selling jellied eels, winkles and mussels in vinegar. Most Belgian charcuteries sell this salad ready-made. I remember one day in Brussels buying finger-long giant mussels, tender and meaty, bathed in a white sauce speckled with green parsley, and eating it straight away in the street, undaunted by the reproving looks I got from passers-by.

In winter, for an informal week-end lunch party, I serve this salad with prawns, pieces of smoked eel, *taramaroussia* (p. 55) and fillets of smoked mackerel accompanied by plenty of hot toast and the best Devon butter, and in the centre of the table an enormous china bowl of mixed green salad crowning it all.

3 tubs of mussels in vinegar	I generous teaspoon of French
I small pot of sour cream	mustard
I bunch of parsley, washed and	salt and pepper to taste
coarsely chopped	cayenne pepper for decoration

Drain the mussels. Blend together the sour cream, most of the parsley, the mustard, salt and pepper. Mix with the drained mussels. Dust with cayenne pepper and sprinkle with the rest of the parsley. Refrigerate until ready to serve.

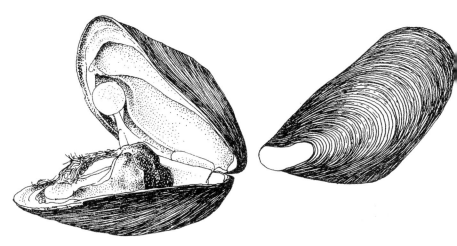

TARAMAROUSSIA

Normally tarama has garlic (which detracts from the taste of the cod's roe) and soaked bread (which destroys the delicate texture of the tiny grains). Never replace the fresh smoked cod's roe with roe from a jar: it is much too salty. I prefer to buy a few pieces in winter and freeze them until needed.

about 250-g/8-oz piece of smoked cod's roe	a pinch of cayenne pepper
juice of 1 lemon	a pinch of ground ginger
150 ml/¼ pint double cream	paprika

In this recipe it is important not to use a blender or food processor but to mix with a fork, in order to keep the little eggs whole.

With a sharp knife, slit open the skin of the cod's roe and empty it into a bowl with the help of a little spoon. Pour over half of the lemon juice and mash very thoroughly with a fork, breaking all the lumps. Repeat the operation with the other half of the lemon juice. Beat the cream in gradually. At this stage don't worry if the mixture is too runny, as after a few minutes the lemon will have soured the cream and the taramaroussia will be set. Season to your taste with the cayenne pepper and the ginger. No salt is needed. Transfer to a serving bowl and dust with paprika. Refrigerate.

Serve with pitta bread melba. Toast the pitta on both sides, slit in half while still warm and brown the untoasted insides.

〜

GRAVAD LAX

Fish pickled in this manner is, to my taste, superior to commercially smoked fish. The flesh is more moist and less salty. The method works equally well with whole salmon, salmon trout or mackerel. It is essential to use fresh dill; dried dill weed won't do. Saltpetre is now difficult to obtain so if you can't find it don't worry. It just helps keep the flesh bright pink instead of slightly grayish. Serve with a mustard sauce (p. 138-9).

1½ tablespoons coarse salt	1 kg/2 lb whole salmon, trout or
1½ tablespoons caster sugar	mackerel
1 teaspoon black peppercorns,	bunch of fresh dill
lightly crushed	small glass of brandy (optional)
pinch of saltpetre (optional)	

Mix the salt, sugar, pepper and saltpetre, if used, together in a small bowl. Bone the fish (or ask your fishmonger to do this for you). Divide it into 2 fillets and wipe off any moisture. Then rub the mixed seasoning into it. Chop the dill, stalks and all. Lay one third of it in a china dish and place on top the first fillet, skin side down. Cover with a little more dill, then place the second fillet on top, skin side up. Pour over the brandy if used. Cover the dish with foil and a board that just fits inside the dish. Weight it down heavily. Leave in the refrigerator to pickle for at least 48 hours. (You can leave it up to 5 days.) Before serving, wipe off all the marinade and slice very thin, as you would for smoked fish.

SMOKED SALMON ROULEAUX

Ricotta is an unsalted Italian cheese (traditionally made from sheep or buffalo milk) which looks like cottage or cream cheese, and has a distinctive fresh flavour. As the name ('recooked') implies, it is the product of repeated slow boiling of milk from which the butter fat has been extracted. Ricotta is very perishable, even when refrigerated, and should be eaten within 24–48 hours. It is now made in England from cow's milk and is available from Italian grocers, who are supplied daily with whole basket-shaped ricotta cheeses.

Ricotta is firm and at the same time moist. The salmon will therefore adhere to the filling and make neat *rouleaux* (pancakes), even with irregular slices.

250 g/8 oz ricotta cheese
handful of chopped parsley (the
flat leaf sort preferably) and
some sprigs
salt

pepper
about 8 very thin slices smoked
salmon
dry dill weeds

Mash the ricotta and the chopped parsley with a large fork. Season with the pepper and a very little salt.

Take a slice of smoked salmon, lay it flat, spoon some of the ricotta mixture over one end and roll sausage-like. Repeat the operation until all the *rouleaux* are formed. Place on a rectangular cake dish, if you have one. (My green Provençal one looks beautiful with the contrasting salmon colour and the white filling showing at the sides.) Decorate with a few sprigs of parsley, and sprinkle with a little dill.

SMOKED HADDOCK RAMEKINS

In this recipe, the haddock is not cooked and retains a delicate smoky taste. The texture is smooth and creamy. The orange tinge of the fish is more evident with the addition of saffron. You will save time if you have a food processor, but otherwise follow the method using a pestle and mortar. Serve with crisp rye biscuits.

a little saffron
3 tablespoons olive oil
about 4 tablespoons
single cream
500 g/1 lb smoked haddock

a few drops of lemon juice
white pepper
1 tablespoon dried fennel seeds
or 1 tablespoon fresh fennel
leaves, chopped

Pound the saffron stigmas in a mortar and put into a small jug with the oil and cream. Leave for about 10 minutes.

Remove skin and bones from the smoked haddock, and cut into medium-sized pieces. In a food processor pound half of the fish, turning on and off continually for about 30 seconds. Scrape down with a spatula and add the lemon juice and remaining haddock. Process again until all is evenly chopped. With the machine running, gradually pour the oil and cream through the funnel. Process until completely smooth. Taste for seasoning – normally salt is not necessary. The mixture should have a soft, but not runny consistency. Divide it between 6 ramekins. Decorate with fennel seeds or chopped fresh fennel leaves. I serve these ramekins at room temperature, but if you prefer they may be refrigerated.

STEAMED GREY MULLET

This dish is a good example of how you can use steaming baskets for the whole main course: one basket for the fish, and two for the vegetables. Though the whole process seems complicated, it is in fact simple and doesn't require much washing up, as there is no need to transfer to a serving dish. Bring to the table with the saffron and garlic mayonnaise described below.

UTENSILS

a wok with standing ring, or any pan large enough to take the baskets
three 30-cm/12-inch Chinese bamboo steaming baskets and one lid
one round heatproof dish, about 30 cm/11 inches in diameter and
rather shallow to fit inside one basket, or failing this some foil
First read the note on using bamboo steaming baskets (p. 91).

1 grey mullet, weighing about 1–1½ kg/2–3 lb	about 20 tiny new potatoes
1 small onion	about 20 mint leaves
6 very large mushrooms of even size and shape	3 tablespoons sour cream
	a few drops of sesame oil
½ small fennel head	sea salt
	pepper

Clean the gutted fish under cold, running water and pat dry. Season the inside. Chop coarsely the onion, the mushroom stalks and the fennel top leaves, and put them in the cavity. Arrange the fish, curling it to fit, in the greased heatproof dish (or piece of foil). Put inside one basket.

Wash and pat dry the unpeeled potatoes. Slice each in two lengthways, season with sea salt and pepper. Place one mint leaf between the halves, re-form and put them in a basket.

Wipe the mushroom caps and lay them upside down in the third basket. Spoon a little sour cream in the centre of each. Dribble a few drops of sesame oil in the gills. Dust with salt and pepper. Pile a little of the finely chopped fennel in the centre of each mushroom.

Fill the wok three-quarters full with water. Put it on its ring and bring to the boil. Fit the fish basket on the wok and steam, covered, for 15 minutes. Then place on top of it the mushroom and potato baskets, putting the lid on the top basket, and steam for about 20 minutes longer.

If the fish was cooked on a piece of foil transfer it to a serving dish but bring the vegetables to the table in their baskets with a plate underneath them.

Serve with courgette and walnut salad (p. 123).

SAFFRON AND GARLIC MAYONNAISE

To 250 ml/½ pint of homemade mayonnaise add half a garlic clove, crushed, and 5 saffron stigmas which have previously been powdered in a mortar.

MAQUEREAUX À LA MOUTARDE

Mackerel is a smooth-scaled sea fish which catches the eye on the fishmonger's stall with its striped, iridescent colouring. Some people find that the mackerel's strong smell invades the kitchen during cooking, but it is not offensive when cooked in this way. The mustardy sauce works well with the gamy taste of the fish. I like to serve it with sweet and sour gooseberry sauce (p. 140) as a side dish.

3 medium-sized mackerel	juice of 1 lemon
250 ml/½ pint crème fraîche	2 tablespoons chopped parsley
(p. 16) or 125 ml/¼ pint each	1 lemon and 1 orange, sliced
single and double cream	sea salt and white pepper
3 tablespoons strong French	60 g/2 oz butter
mustard	

Ask your fishmonger to gut the mackerel, leaving the heads on. Wash them briefly and pat dry with a paper towel. Place the fish in a greased ovenproof dish (use an attractive one which can be brought to the table). Stir the mustard with the crème fraîche or cream. Add the lemon juice and parsley. Season, being sparing with the salt. Pour the sauce over the mackerel. Decorate each fish with a slice of lemon overlapping a slice of orange. Dot with bits of butter and bake in a pre-heated oven at gas 5–6/375°–400°F/190°–200°C for 25 minutes. The cream sauce should have reduced a little and be lightly browned on the top.

THE SELFISH SOLE

To my mind, this is typical nursery cooking: a truly simple idea, but with a perfect result. As a child, it always seemed to me miraculous that the fish was cooked through the plates. Nowadays, if I am alone, I prepare a sole using this method; it makes me remember and smile. Eat with a watercress salad and boubou potatoes (p. 110) accompanied by the fresh coriander sauce (p. 139).

1 lemon sole	white pepper
a nut of butter	¼ lemon
salt	

Take two meat plates large enough to hold the fish easily (with head and tail, of course). Have ready a saucepan of boiling water. The pan should be a little smaller than the plates. Smear the plates with butter, sandwich the fish between them, the top plate bottom up. Fit on the top of the saucepan, and steam for 15 minutes. Remove the top plate with oven gloves. Bring the sole to the table on its hot plate. Season with salt and white pepper, and sharpen with a squeeze of lemon.

BACALHAU-BRAZ

This dish is often served in Brazil and Portugal, and though similar to the French *stofinato* on p. 62, it is more substantial as the ingredients include potatoes and onions. I buy the salt cod from Italian grocers who usually stock it. It keeps up to a month in a refrigerator, but make sure it is well wrapped.

The way the ingredients are cut is important here, as the shape, strangely enough, gives a texture which is unique to this dish.

500 g/1 lb salt cod	3–4 medium potatoes peeled
3 tablespoons olive oil	and cut in long sticks
2 medium-sized onions, cut in	1 garlic clove
long, thin strips	5 eggs, lightly beaten

I handful black olives (sweet,   a little parsley, coarsely chopped
    herbed ones are best)   freshly ground pepper

Soak the salt cod in cold water for 24 hours, changing the water several times. After a last rinse, pat dry and cut in thin strips, discarding any bones. Reserve.

Heat the olive oil in a large heavy omelette pan and fry the onions until they are lightly browned, but not yet completely transparent. Add the potatoes, the cod and the crushed garlic. After 15 minutes, check that the potatoes are cooked, but still holding their shape. Pour over the lightly beaten eggs. Throw over the olives, and sprinkle with the parsley. Season with freshly ground pepper (no salt is necessary). When the omelette is brown underneath, slide onto a serving dish. Serve very hot, cut in wedges like a cake.

STOFINATO

I first discovered this dish in the Auvergne, where walnut trees are plentiful and their oil is no extravagance.

500 g/1 lb salt cod   125 ml/¼ pint single cream
3 tablespoons walnut oil   a little parsley, chopped fine
    1 clove of garlic   pepper
    4 eggs lightly beaten

Soak the salt cod for 24 hours, changing the cold water 2 or 3 times. After a last rinse, pat dry and slice in thin strips, discarding any bones.

Heat the walnut oil in a frying pan and when very hot, but not smoking, add the strips of cod and stir constantly with a wooden spoon. The oil will become a white purée as the fish disintegrates into it. At this stage add the crushed garlic. Have ready the eggs and the cream, beaten together in a small bowl. Pour them quickly over the fish, and proceed as you would for a normal omelette. When the eggs are just set, but the mixture still creamy, sprinkle the parsley on the top. Transfer to a serving dish and serve at once with a little freshly ground pepper on top.

MONKFISH WATERZOOI

Waterzooi is a Flemish dish made with chicken or fish. In this version I omit the white wine and butter, and use monkfish. Only the tail, which has a lobster-like texture, is sold for consumption. In Belgium they use the green celery which is the top of celeriac, but as it is not available here I use English white celery.

This dish takes the place of both soup and main course. It has the firm flesh of the fish combined with the small, delicate-tasting pieces of vegetables. The cream sauce binds together all the ingredients in a rich yet light broth. Serve in soup plates.

TO SERVE 8

2 kg/4 lb monkfish on the bone
1 litre/2 pints water plus thyme, bay leaf, peppercorns, parsley stalks
½ stick celery, chopped fine
500 g/1 lb leeks, cut in 2-cm/¾-inch slices

500 g/1 lb carrots, cut in julienne strips
500 ml/1 pint double cream
3 egg yolks
a handful chopped parsley
salt and pepper

Make a stock with the water, herbs, salt, pepper and bone. After cooking, discard the herbs and bone and put into the boiling stock the fish cut in large chunks and the prepared vegetables. Cook on a low heat for 20 minutes. Meanwhile, whip together the cream and egg yolks until the mixture looks like a thick, yellow custard. When the fish and vegetables are ready, take off the heat and stir in the creamy sauce. Adjust the seasoning, add the parsley and serve at once, ladling a little of the fish, vegetables and sauce into warmed plates. Present at the same time a basket of steamed new potatoes, kept warm wrapped in a napkin with corners folded over.

SMOKED OYSTERS STEAMED IN VINE LEAVES

Vine leaves used like this taste quite different from Greek *dolmades*, which is the way they are usually known. Here they impart a woody flavour to the filling. It is best to get dried fungi for this recipe; their smoky taste goes well with oysters.

About 20 vine leaves (kept in brine)	2 tins smoked oysters
250 g/8 oz fresh spinach, washed	2 tablespoons fresh coriander, chopped
1 tablespoon butter	2 tablespoons spring onion, chopped
250 g/8 oz ricotta cheese	½ teaspoon ground mace
10–12 dried fungi or 4 medium-sized mushrooms	cayenne pepper
	salt

Soak the vine leaves in cold water for about 1 hour. Rinse them under a cold tap, unfold the creases and drain on paper towels, rough side up.

Sauté the clean spinach in the butter for a few minutes. It should be just wilted and remain a bright emerald colour. Chop very fine and reserve.

In a bowl, break the ricotta with a fork and add the chopped dried fungi or mushrooms, smoked oysters, fresh coriander, spring onion and spinach. Season with mace, cayenne and salt. Chill for at least 1 hour. (Up to this stage the recipe may be prepared ahead of time.)

To assemble, put a little of the filling in the centre of one leaf, roll the stem end over it, fold down the sides and roll tightly towards the point of the leaf. Lay, seam down, in a bamboo steaming basket (see method p.92). Repeat the operation with all the leaves. Set the basket over a pan of boiling water, cover with the lid and steam for about 20 minutes. Remove from the heat, using an oven cloth so that the steam doesn't burn your hands. Serve at once in the steaming baskets.

PAGLIA E FIENO
WITH SMOKED SALMON

The literal translation of *paglia e fieno* is 'straw and hay', appropriate for this mixture of yellow and green pasta. I like the informality of the large, shallow china bowl put in the centre of the table, so that guests can help themselves. The pinkish hue of the smoked salmon added to the pasta duo makes the dish even more enticing.

  Making pasta is great fun and so easy with a machine. Because of its increasing popularity, pasta machine prices have dropped by nearly half in the last few years. Making pasta with a machine takes about 1 hour if you are in a hurry, or 3 hours if you make a real event of it, having children and friends to help. Everyone gets much pleasure from pulling the long sheets of coloured dough, rolled to a satin-smooth texture. Then the cutters are adjusted to make strands of the required width: you may want tagliatelle, fettuccine or lasagne. Finally the pasta is dried on a bamboo pole (bought from a garden shop) which is held between two chairs; backs placed apart.

YELLOW PASTA

300 g/10 oz unbleached flour	½ tablespoon olive oil
3 large eggs, at room temperature	table salt
	a pinch of saffron (optional)

GREEN PASTA

300 g/10 oz unbleached flour	1 teaspoon olive oil
2 large eggs at room temperature	table salt
250 g/8 oz packet frozen leaf spinach	a pinch of mace (optional)

YELLOW PASTA

Place the flour in a mound on a pastry board. Make a well in the centre and put in the eggs, olive oil, salt and saffron (if used). With a fork, first mix together the yolks, whites, oil, salt and spice, then begin to incorporate the flour from the inner rim of the well, always incorporating fresh flour from the lower part, and pushing it under the dough to keep the dough from sticking to the board. When half of the flour has been absorbed, start kneading, always using the palms of your hands. Continue working in the flour until it is all incorporated. Leave to rest for 15 minutes or as long as 2 hours. This helps to relax the gluten and makes the dough easier to work.

Attach the machine to your table by tightening the clamp at the bottom. Set the wheel for the rollers at the widest setting. Take about a third of the pasta and pass it through the plain rollers. After the pasta has come out from between the rollers in a roughly rectangular strip, fold this in three so that the width remains the same while the length is a third of what it was. Sprinkle with flour and repeat the operation about 10 times; by then it will be obvious to the eye that the dough has become a properly smooth, homogeneous mixture. (These steps take the place of hand kneading.) Flour the pastry board and lay the first strip on it. Repeat the operation with the rest of the pasta.

Move the wheel to the next number in order to bring the rollers a little closer. Now pass the three sheets of dough one by one through the rollers. After each sheet of pasta has passed once through the machine with the rollers in this position you should bring the rollers closer together by turning the adjusting wheel. Every now and then it will be necessary to cut the dough in two across, because otherwise the sheets become so long that they are difficult to handle. Stop at the required thickness. (I stop at the number before the last.) Lay the sheets of pasta on a floured table, cover with tea-cloths and leave to rest for 10–15 minutes. Meanwhile, set a broom handle or a bamboo pole (about 1 metre/1½ yards long) on the backs of two chairs placed the right distance apart.

The pasta is now ready to be cut to the shape of your choice. Set the

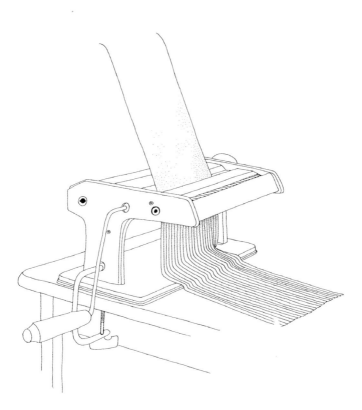

cutters for tagliatelle or fettuccine. (Fettuccine is the Roman version of the Bolognese tagliatelle, but is normally a little narrower and thicker.) Pass through the cutters and hang over the broom handle or bamboo pole, making sure that the pasta strands do not overlap. Leave to dry. If you think that you have made too much of it, put some in the refrigerator (where it will keep for a few days) or freeze.

GREEN PASTA

In a small saucepan, heat the thawed spinach and the salt. Simmer for a few minutes. Drain and leave to cool. Wrap the spinach in a cheese cloth and squeeze out as much liquid as possible. With a sharp knife, chop the spinach very fine. Add to the eggs and proceed as above.

THE SAUCE

250 ml/½ pint crème fraîche (p. 16) or 125 ml/¼ pint each single and sour cream	small bunch parsley, chopped fine
	1 sprig tarragon or 1 teaspoon dried
250 g/8 oz smoked salmon, cut in julienne strips (trimmings are fine for this)	freshly ground pepper paprika 3 tablespoons oil

Put the cream and salmon in a bowl and leave for an hour or so. The smoked fish will swell and soften a little and impart its flavour to the cream. Then add all the other ingredients. Check the seasoning, and keep at room temperature until needed.

Have ready a warmed serving dish. Fill a very large pan with water. Bring to the boil, add 1 tablespoon coarse salt and 1 tablespoon oil (this will prevent the pasta from sticking together). Put in the fresh pasta and boil for 3–5 minutes. Test one strand: it should be *al dente*, that is to say cooked, but a little firm to the tooth. Drain in a colander. Transfer to the serving dish. Toss in 2 tablespoons of oil and then the sauce with the smoked salmon. Lastly, add the chopped herbs. Serve at once.

Any left over is delicious eaten cold as a salad.

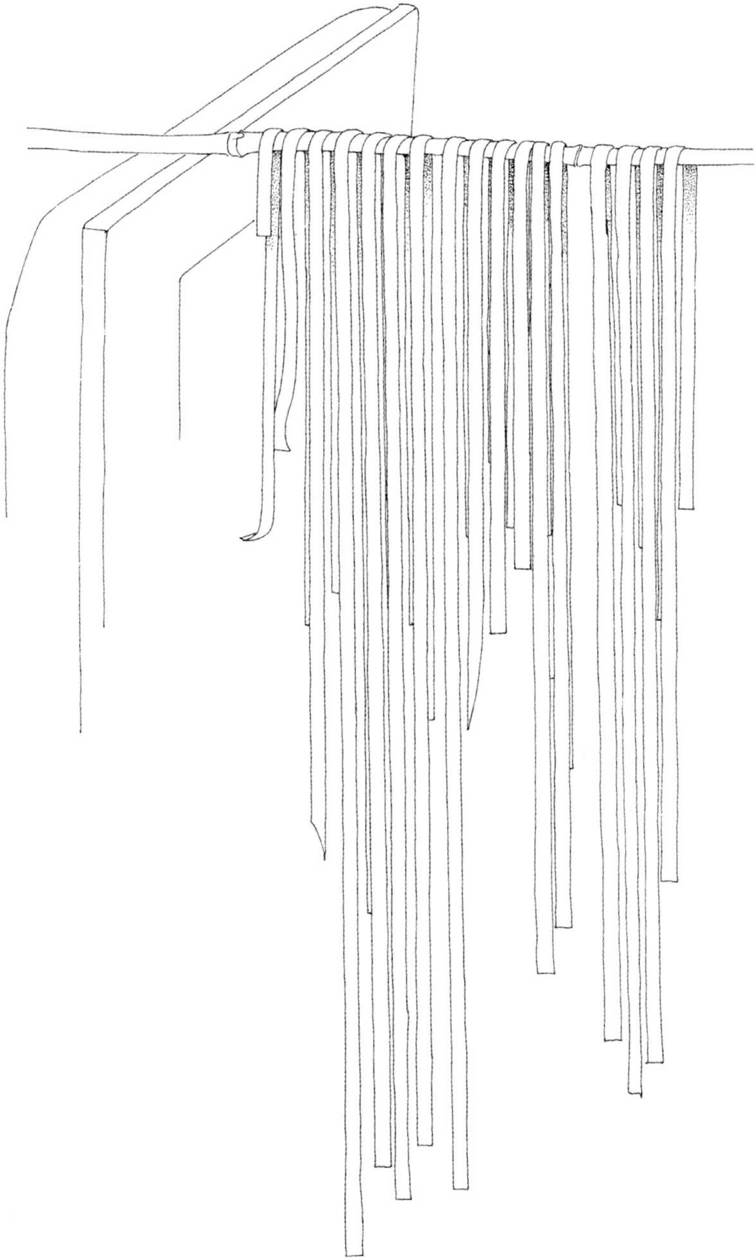

POULTRY
AND GAME

POULET BAMAKO

The lemon juice cooks the chicken pieces and the long marinating time makes the flesh tender and delicately flavoured. The bacon prevents the chicken from getting dry and adds a crispness to the dish. Sometimes I reserve the skin and cut it into bite-sized bits which are deep-fried like the French *grattons*, which we eat while having our drinks.

Serve with vegetable couscous (p. 111).

1 large chicken, cut in 12 pieces (or 6 thighs and 6 breasts)	dried herbs: blend of thyme, rosemary, bay leaves, tarragon,
juice of 6 lemons	parsley, sage
4 cm/2 inches fresh ginger, chopped fine	12 slices smoky bacon, cut paper-thin
2 garlic cloves	2 tablespoons olive oil
salt and black pepper	

Skin the chicken pieces (reserve the skin if you are making *grattons*). In a large glass or enamelled bowl, combine the chicken, lemon juice, fresh ginger, whole garlic cloves (crushed, but not peeled), salt and pepper. Leave to marinate, covered, overnight.

Drain the chicken pieces. (The marinade may be used with the pan juices to make a lemony gravy, which is served separately in a sauce boat.) Have ready a soup plate containing the seasoned herbs. Take a chicken piece, roll it in the herbs, wrap around with a slice of bacon, secure with a cocktail stick and lay on an oiled oven dish. Repeat the operation until all the pieces are done and brush over with olive oil.

Bake for 30–40 minutes at gas 6/400°F/200°C. Arrange the chicken pieces on a china dish, surrounding the couscous. The dish is also good eaten cold for a picnic.

POULET À LA CROÛTE AU SEL

The first time I tried this method of cooking, I must confess, I was apprehensive and sceptical about the result. In this recipe the chicken is enclosed in a highly salted dough which during cooking will work as a hermetic container and allow the bird to be cooked to perfection; the flesh will be tender and moist, the skin crisp and golden, and with the added aroma of the salt and herbs.

2–2½ kg/4–5 lb chicken	1 onion
750 g/1½ lb sea salt	1 sprig thyme
750/1½ lb flour	1 sprig rosemary
a scant 500 ml/pint water	salt and pepper

Pre-heat the oven to gas 7/425°F/220°C.

Put the peeled whole onion and sprig of thyme in the seasoned cavity of the chicken. Make a few slits in the thighs and breasts and insert in each a little rosemary. Reserve.

In a large bowl, make a smooth dough with the sea salt, flour and water. Roll it out on a lightly floured wooden board or marble slab. (The pastry should be large enough to enclose the chicken.) Wrap the bird in the dough, making sure that it is well sealed. Place the chicken on an oven tray and bake in the pre-heated oven for $1\frac{1}{2}$ to $1\frac{2}{3}$ hours.

When ready put the chicken on a wooden board and bring to the table. With a short bladed knife, cut a 'hat' into the crust, large enough to remove the chicken easily and cut into pieces. Discard all the crust. Serve with potted carrots (p. 104), and chicken liver dressing (p. 142).

BLANKETED CHICKEN

The blanket is a stuffing which is inserted between the skin and the flesh of the bird. When the chicken is sliced, it is very juicy and has a pretty green border. You should use whole baby carrots, the size of your little finger.

1.5-kg/3-lb *poulet de Bresse*
(the sort which has been
fed with corn and has yellow,
flavourful flesh)

1 onion
500 g/1 lb tiny new carrots,
scrubbed
olive oil

STUFFING

175 g/6 oz cream cheese
3 tablespoons fresh chives,
chopped
4 tablespoons fresh parsley,
chopped

2-cm/1-inch piece crystallised
ginger, chopped finely
1 teaspoon mixed peel
freshly grated nutmeg
salt
freshly ground pepper

Mix thoroughly all the ingredients for the 'blanket'. Fill the 2 halves of a chicken brick (see the next recipe) with water and leave to soak for 10 minutes. Loosen the skin of the chicken on the breast and thighs with the handle of a spoon. Spread the filling between flesh and skin, patting it with your hands to make an even layer. Insert the peeled, whole onion in the cavity. Rub the skin with olive oil. Empty the water from the brick, line the bottom half with foil (this makes it easier to clean afterwards). Lay the chicken inside, surrounded by the carrots; cover with top half of the brick, and bake in the oven at gas 9/475°F/240°C for about 1 hour.

PHEASANT WITH POIVRE VERT

Nowadays people seem to arrive later and later for dinner. I used to fuss about the time we should start eating, but now I get everything ready beforehand. All that is left is to arrange the food on serving dishes, toss the salad and light the candles.

One of the advantages of using the clay brick for poultry and game is that, even overcooked, the bird will stay tender and moist. Twenty minutes' delay is no problem. At its worst, a pheasant will be like Peking duck, falling apart but still flavourful and juicy.

Very little fat is required in this recipe. The stuffing will impart its taste to the bird, and the vegetables will cook in the natural juice of the meat, with an added smoky taste given by clay-baking.

1 large pheasant	2 small parsnips
2 bacon rashers	salt and pepper
4 medium-sized mushrooms	a little thyme

FOR THE STUFFING

4 bacon rashers	10 green peppercorns
2 small onions, chopped finely	a little powdered mace
125 g/4 oz cream cheese	1 teaspoon thyme

First fill the 2 halves of a chicken brick with cold water and leave to soak for about 10 minutes. The porous clay will absorb the water which will be converted into steam during cooking, preventing the pheasant from getting dry.

In a non-stick frying pan, cook 4 rashers of bacon until crisp. Drain on a paper towel and chop. Reserve. In the bacon fat, sauté the chopped onions until soft and transparent. Mash the cream cheese with the green peppercorns, the mace and thyme. Add the bacon and onions.

Clean and wipe dry the inside of the pheasant. Over a flame, burn the remaining feathers. Fill the cavity with the stuffing. With a piece of

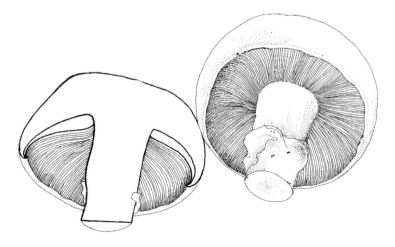

string, tie the legs together. Cover the top of the bird with the 2 rashers of bacon left.

Line the bottom half of the chicken brick with foil (this makes cleaning easier afterwards). Put in the pheasant. Surround with the sliced mushrooms and the coarsely chopped parsnips. Season with salt and pepper and a little thyme. Cover with the other half of the brick.

Put in the oven turned to gas 9/475°F/240°C and cook for 1 hour or a little longer. About 10 minutes before the end of the cooking, you may remove the top of the brick to brown the pheasant's skin.

Transfer to a serving dish, carve and surround with the vegetables and some of the juice. Scoop out some of the stuffing for each helping.

GROUSE WITH QUINCES

While reading Greek cookery books, I came across several recipes using quinces with meat dishes. I tried quinces with grouse and found their tartness an interesting and clean counterpart to the strength of the game.

2 grouse	150 ml/¼ pint orange juice
4 bacon rashers	1 cinnamon stick (optional)
125 g/4 oz butter	salt and freshly ground pepper
4 quinces	

Have the grouse prepared and dressed with the bacon. Cut the quinces in quarters (after washing them to remove the fluff) and cut out the hard centre, but do not peel them. Cut the quarters into thick slices and fry them in 2 tablespoons of the butter, until they begin to soften (about 15 minutes).

In a heavy cast-iron casserole, melt the remaining butter; when it starts foaming add the grouse and sauté on both sides until golden. Add the orange juice, stick of cinnamon (if used), salt and pepper. Cover and cook on low heat for 1 to 1¼ hours (depending on the size of the grouse), turning the birds once or twice to ensure even browning. Add the quinces half-way through the cooking. Before serving, remove the cinnamon stick, carve the grouse and lay on a dish surrounded with the quinces and coated with the juices.

QUAILS IN VINE LEAVES

Nowadays, quails found in shops are reared commercially, which means that they are no longer a wild extravagance. They are sold already dressed and may be deep-frozen successfully, but it is important to make sure that the game has been properly hung first.

In this recipe, the quails are wrapped in vine leaves, like little parcels, and spit-roasted. They go well with the grape and radish salad (p. 126).

salt	10 juniper berries, crushed in a
freshly ground pepper	mortar
6 quails	12 vine leaves (bought from
1 teaspoon lemon juice	Greek grocers)
150 g/5 oz butter	6 slices stale white bread, fried

Mix a little salt and freshly ground pepper in a saucer, then dip your fingers in the mixture and rub the quails all over, inside and out. Beat together lemon juice and butter, add the crushed juniper, and season to taste. Put a knob of the butter in the cavity of each quail; spread the remaining butter all over the outside. Wrap each bird with 2 vine leaves and secure with string. Before cooking, leave the birds in the refrigerator for 2 hours to let the flavours mix.

If you are using an oven rotisserie, pre-heat the oven to gas 7/425°F/220°C. Place the fried bread slices in a foil-lined tin under the birds. This will collect the tasty drippings. Cook for 20 minutes or until juices run clear when the quails are pierced with a thin skewer around the inside leg area, where the meat is thickest. Serve each quail resting on a piece of the fried bread.

SOUPS

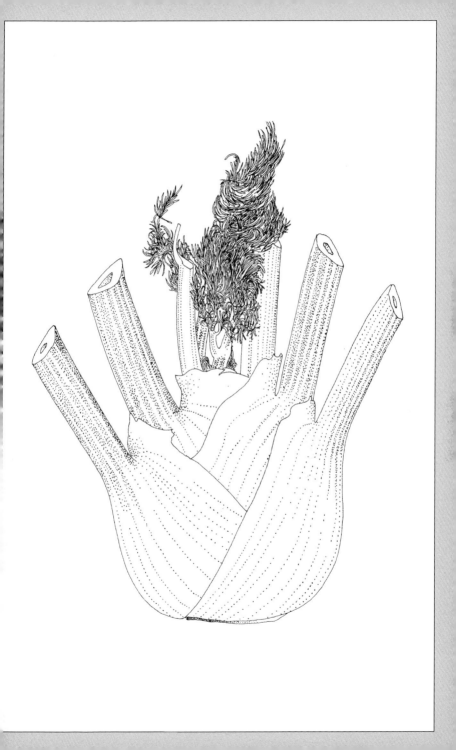

JELLIED WATERCRESS AND APPLE SOUP

I can't see why we have such unbreakable rules for the order in which we serve dishes. Why not have this refreshing, soothing soup to follow a hot, spicy dish as the Chinese do, often ending a meal with a light broth to clean the palate. For decoration, instead of the cream and chives, you can embed one brilliant red nasturtium flower in each serving of soup. To accompany the soup, toast (rather than fry) some pappadums under a grill and pile them in a wicker basket.

4 bunches watercress	gelatine
375 ml/1½ pints chicken stock	3 Granny Smith apples
1 teaspoon salt	juice of ½ lemon
black pepper	125 ml/¼ pint sour cream
1 packet (½ tablespoon)	fresh chives

Trim the long stems from the watercress and discard them. Chop the leaves and remaining stems and put them in a heavy enamel saucepan. Add stock, salt and pepper. Bring the mixture to the boil and cook it over low heat for 30 minutes. Take a cupful of the very hot stock and dissolve the gelatine in it, stirring briskly for a few minutes. Liquidise the soup in a blender and add the strained gelatine-stock mixture. Transfer to a bowl, and when partly cooled, chill for several hours.

Coarsely grate the unpeeled apples (discarding the core) and toss in the lemon juice. Serve in small individual bowls as follows: put at the bottom 1 tablespoon of grated apple, then spoon over some of the wobbly watercress soup, which should be set a little but not firm. Top with a dollop of sour cream. Decorate with snipped chives.

COURGETTE AND COCONUT SOUP

This soup is speckled with the green of the courgettes. They impart a fresh taste which is enhanced by the delicate sourness of the buttermilk. The coconut gives a faint sweetness to the soup. During the summer, we take a large thermos of this soup on picnics.

6–8 courgettes
250 ml/½ pint chicken stock (or ½ cube dissolved in 250 ml/½ pint water)

3 tablespoons desiccated coconut
250 ml/½ pint buttermilk
salt and pepper
a little fresh parsley

Trim but do not peel the courgettes. After washing and slicing them, put in a pan with the stock. Bring to the boil, reduce the heat and simmer, covered for about 20 minutes. Stir in the desiccated coconut for the last 5 minutes and season with salt and pepper. Leave to cool completely.

Strain and purée the courgettes in a blender. The stock is reserved for the final step. In a tureen, stir together the cooled stock and the buttermilk, add the courgettes. Blend well. Adjust the seasoning if necessary. Scatter the chopped parsley on top and chill.

Serve with warm banana bread (p.42).

BEETROOT AND FENNEL SOUP

This is a refreshing soup of the most gorgeous colour, ruby-like with a white dollop of cream and green fennel leaves on the top. The two vegetables are an unexpectedly happy combination: they complement each other well.

The outer stalks of a head of celery are a good substitute for the fennel. Yogurt may replace the sour cream.

2–3 cooked beetroots
1 medium-sized head of fennel
250 ml/½ pint chicken stock

125 ml/¼ pint sour cream
pepper and salt
fennel leaves to decorate

Peel, chop and liquidise the cooked beetroot. Put in a large bowl and reserve.

Cut the fennel in large chunks and put in a saucepan. Just cover with the stock and cook with the lid on for about 20 minutes. Drain the fennel. Liquidise alone in a blender until smooth. Add to the beetroot purée together with the stock. Taste for seasoning. Stir and chill.

Just before serving, spoon over a little sour cream, and lastly decorate with the reserved fennel leaves.

CRÈME D'AVOCAT AU CUMIN

This soup is so simple to make that I almost feel embarrassed when friends ask for the recipe. It is a real cheat, since it uses tinned consommé. The texture is smooth but full-bodied, the colour is a delicate, pale green that is prevented from discolouring by the lemon juice and by leaving one of the stones inside the tureen until serving time. The liquid smoke adds an intriguing taste to this delicious soup.

3 medium-sized avocado pears
2 tins Campbell's clear beef
consommé
1 tablespoon lemon juice
250 ml/½ pint yogurt

paprika
salt
a few drops liquid smoke (see
note p. 136)
2 teaspoons cumin seeds

Blend the peeled and stoned avocados (reserving one stone for the tureen) and consommé. Stir in the yogurt and lemon. Season with paprika, salt and smoke. Add half the cumin seeds and chill, covered, for several hours. Serve in small cups, decorating with the remaining cumin seeds and a little more paprika.

Serve with toasted potato and caraway bread (p. 41).

POTAGE BATWINIA

This is a Russian soup with a clean and fresh taste. It seems that the Russians have a predilection for beetroot in soup, but for this recipe it is the leaves which are used. They are a deep green streaked with burgundy, and, by the way, are much richer in vitamins than the roots. They are simply delicious steamed and served with lemon quarters and fresh butter. Choose young, fresh beetroot leaves.

Batwinia is normally made with *kvass*, a fizzy, mildly alcoholic drink made from rye bread and fermented yeast, but I use instead a dry sparkling white wine.

2 bunches of sorrel
about 250 g/8 oz beetroot leaves
250 g/8 oz spinach
2 pickled dill cucumbers, chopped very fine
1 tablespoon fresh dill, chopped fine (or 1 teaspoon dried)
1 tablespoon fresh tarragon, chopped fine (or 1 teaspoon dried)

250 ml/½ pint dry white wine, chilled
250 ml/½ pint cold water
½ teaspoon caster sugar
salt and white pepper
ice cubes
2 tablespoons grated horseradish
2 tablespoons tarragon vinegar
about 250 g/8 oz cooked salmon (optional)

Stem and thoroughly wash the sorrel, beetroot and spinach leaves. Put them all in a pan without liquid, except the water still clinging to the leaves. Cover and cook slowly over low heat for about 10 minutes, stirring occasionally. Cool.

In a small bowl put the finely chopped dill cucumbers and herbs and two ice cubes. Cover and chill.

Purée the cooled greens in a blender, or rub through a fine sieve with a wooden spoon. Add the white wine and water and stir well. Season with salt, pepper and sugar. Chill until ready to serve.

To serve, put the soup in delicate china soup cups, placing an ice cube and a little piece of the fish (if used) in each one. Garnish with the

pickled cucumber and herb mixture. Pass around a little bowl with the
horseradish stirred in the vinegar.

SMOKED TROUT SOUP

A very unusual soup, rich and delicate at the same time. A perfect
collation after the theatre when you want something nourishing, but
not too heavy if you go to bed straight afterwards. Of course it can be
made ahead of time, indeed it is better left for a while so that the flavour
matures.

It looks sumptuous if you serve it in frosted glass cups. Have on the
side some pumpernickel bread buttered and cut in long fingers.

2 smoked trout	4 tablespoons vodka
2 tins clear beef consommé	2 tablespoons sour cream
4 tablespoons grated	dusting of paprika, fresh
horseradish	chopped dill
10 drops Tabasco	

Remove the flesh from the trout, taking great care to discard all the
tiny bones. Blend the trout flesh, the consommé, the horseradish and
Tabasco in the liquidiser for a few minutes. Chill for several hours. Just
before serving, add the vodka and the cream. Serve in glass cups that
you have frosted by leaving them in the freezing compartment of your
refrigerator for a little while. Dust with paprika and dill.

CHAMPAGNE AND STILTON SOUP

This is a rich, luscious soup, ideal for a winter dinner. It looks pretty in
little individual tureens. Flat champagne is perfectly adequate to use.
White bread may be used for the croûtons, but stale corn bread is more
interesting, fried and cut in long fingers.

60 g/2 oz butter
30 g/1 oz flour
250 ml/½ pint milk
125 ml/¼ pint double cream
250 ml/½ pint chicken stock
250 ml/½ pint champagne or
  sparkling dry white wine

1 teaspoon Dijon mustard
250 g/8 oz grated or shredded
  Stilton cheese
nutmeg (optional)
cayenne pepper
fried sticks of corn bread

In a saucepan, melt the butter, add flour and cook the roux over low heat, stirring for several minutes. Pour in gradually the heated milk and cream, beating well with a wooden spoon until smooth and slightly thickened. Add the chicken stock alternately with the champagne. Blend in the mustard. Very carefully, stir in the Stilton, nutmeg (if used), and a little cayenne. When the cheese is just melted, correct the seasoning – normally no salt is needed, but that depends on the initial saltiness of the Stilton.

Serve the soup in heated cups or soup plates. Decorate with more cayenne pepper. In summer I like this soup cold, and add at the last minute a few slices of pear for each serving.

CINDERELLA SOUP

This peasant dish from central France looks quite spectacular when brought to the table, as the pumpkin shell is used in place of a tureen. The fresh walnuts and preserved ginger complement the smooth and bland pumpkin flesh, the walnuts contributing crunchiness and the ginger a spicy lift.

When purchasing the whole pumpkin, remember that it must fit inside your oven. The proportions of cream and milk are left to your discretion.

1 whole pumpkin about 3½ kg/7 lb

4 slices white bread, toasted and cubed

2 handfuls shelled fresh walnuts

1 whole small preserved ginger, chopped finely

125 g/4 oz Gruyère cheese, cubed

enough single cream and milk to three-quarters fill the pumpkin

nutmeg

salt and freshly ground pepper

Cut a lid from the pumpkin and reserve it. With a spoon scoop out the seeds and stringy bits and discard them. Season the cavity well. Put a layer of toasted bread cubes at the bottom, cover with some of the walnuts and half of the chopped ginger. Add part of the cheese. Repeat the operation until all the ingredients are used. Cover slowly with the cream and milk until the pumpkin is three-quarters full. Bake in a moderate oven for about 2 hours. Once or twice during cooking, check the level of the liquid, adding more if necessary, and give a stir to ensure a creamy texture. When ready, serve everyone with a ladle or two of the soup together with some of the softened orange flesh.

VEGETABLES

Over recent years I have discovered several neglected herbs and vegetables. Each time I have a chance to visit a kitchen garden, I am eager to search for something that has almost been forgotten, particularly by city-dwellers like me – such things as sorrel and Swiss chard. Through my enquiries, I have come to the conclusion that often these herbs or vegetables are the easiest to grow and indeed have perhaps been despised for that reason. It has also been rewarding to discover the uses of those parts of familiar plants that are usually discarded, such as beetroot leaves and radish leaves.

In the search for unusual food to delight the senses, the commonest vegetables should not be ignored. The tomato ice which follows is a good example of the unexpected treatment of the familiar, and steaming food in baskets, a method described in this section, not only preserves much of the fresh appearance of vegetables, but also provides an attractive way to present dishes.

TOMATO ICE

Your guests might be surprised to start a meal with an ice, but in Victorian times it was a common custom. In Mrs Marshall's books, *Fancy Ices* and *Book of Ices* (both illustrated with charming woodcuts), savoury ices such as cucumber sorbet, iced spinach à la crème and asparagus sorbet were plentiful.

This ice is wonderfully refreshing and an excellent stimulant for the appetite. I sometimes serve with it nasturtium and avocado salad (p. 151), the texture and colour of which are a perfect contrast to the tomato ice. On these occasions I replace the avocado in this recipe with a bunch of watercress, long stems trimmed.

500 g/1 lb tomatoes, fresh or whole tinned	125 ml/¼ pint sour cream or yogurt
125 ml/¼ pint mayonnaise	juice of 1 lemon

1 teaspoon granulated sugar
1 level tablespoon grated fresh
ginger

1 teaspoon soy sauce
salt and black pepper
2 fairly firm avocados

Skin the tomatoes (if you are using fresh ones) and put them whole into a blender or food processor. Blend until smooth and sieve to remove any remaining seeds. Beat the mayonnaise and sour cream or yogurt; add to the pulped tomatoes. Stir in half the lemon juice, the sugar, grated ginger and soy sauce. Season. Pour into a 500-ml/1-pint ring mould and freeze. An hour before serving, transfer to the refrigerator in order to let the ice soften.

Turn out to serve. Fill the centre with one avocado, cubed and lightly tossed in a little of the remaining lemon juice. Cut the other avocado in long wedges to decorate the outside of the ice ring, brushing them with lemon to prevent discolouring.

STEAMING FOOD IN BAMBOO BASKETS

Bamboo steaming baskets may be found in any town which has a Chinese quarter. Supermarkets there normally sell a whole array of cooking implements as well as food. These baskets are traditionally used for *dim sum*, which are snacks, mainly dumplings, filled with an astonishing repertory of chopped combinations. A *dim sum* meal never includes a big important dish. They are typical of Canton and the surrounding province of Kwangtung.

Bamboo baskets save on heating as you can stack up to 6 baskets of the same size on the top of a pan, and will need only 1 bamboo lid. The most suitable type of pan is enamelled aluminium, with a broad lip and 2 handles. The bottom basket must fit tightly into the rim of the pan in order to prevent the steam escaping. The steam reaching the first basket is of the same temperature as that in the top one.

I use baskets for everyday cooking, not just for exotic dishes. For example, if you are cooking potatoes (cooking time 20 minutes) and broccoli (cooking time 10 minutes), fill the pan with about 8 cm/3 inches of salted water (which may be flavoured with stock, herbs or herb stalks), bring it to the boil, reduce the heat, fit the potato-filled basket with its lid on top of the pan and steam for 10 minutes. At this stage remove the lid, stack your basket of broccoli florets on top of the first basket, put the lid on the top basket and steam for 10 minutes longer. When the time is up, switch off the heat, and, using oven gloves so that the steam does not burn your hands, lift the baskets off the pan and put them on round plates or dishes large enough to hold them.

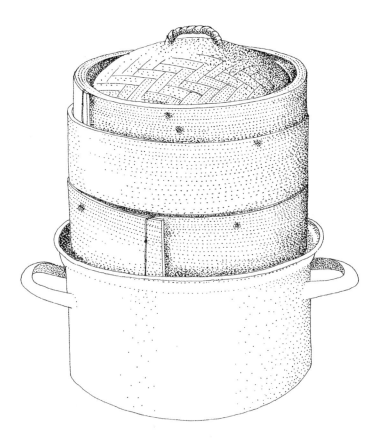

Serve directly from the baskets at the table, using bamboo tongs. If a sauce is to be added to the vegetables, you can serve it separately, or transfer the vegetables to a serving dish. A ricotta and walnut sauce (p. 136) goes particularly well with new potatoes in their skins.

I have given an example for 2 baskets, but you can deal in the same way with 3 or 4 or more baskets. Sometimes I use very small baskets, allowing 1 for each guest. The cooking time is the same, or slightly shorter than when using the boiling method.

The steaming process retains crispness and colour. With some vegetables, particularly broccoli, spinach, French beans, mange-tout peas and Swiss chard, the brightness of the emerald green is enhanced by this method. I have noticed as well that they need less seasoning, as they keep their natural saltiness.

As far as cleaning is concerned, just wipe the bottom of the baskets. I keep them in full view on my kitchen shelves, making a feature of them.

STEAMED HORSE-MUSHROOMS

Cooked in this manner, the mushrooms have a smoky, woody taste. I serve them with small new potatoes, steamed in their skins, and sesame sauce (p. 137).

about 10 large horse-mushrooms	paprika
125 ml/¼ pint sour cream	salt
1 tablespoon sesame oil (or toasted sesame seeds)	pepper

Wipe the mushrooms, and remove the stalks (these can be reserved to flavour a soup). Using 2 large bamboo steaming baskets, put in the mushrooms side by side, top side down. Spoon a little sour cream in the centre of each one, dribble a few drops of the sesame oil or scatter some seeds over the gills, dust with paprika, salt and pepper.

Fill an appropriate pan with 8 cm/3 inches of water; bring to the boil. Fit your bamboo baskets with the lid on the top, and steam for 5–7 minutes. Lift the baskets from the pan with oven gloves on and put them on a plate or round dish. Serve straight from the baskets.

◦~∞~◦

STEAMED BROCCOLI AND CAULIFLOWER FLORETS

I like to leave quite long stems on the broccoli because when steamed they taste very much like asparagus.

I medium-sized cauliflower   500 g/1 lb small broccoli

Trim the ends of the broccoli stems if necessary and cut the cauliflower into florets. Using two 25-cm/10-inch bamboo steaming baskets, arrange the green and white vegetables in a pretty pattern, overlapping them a little in order to show only the tops. Fill the appropriate pan with 8 cm/3 inches of water and bring to the boil. Fit your baskets on the top, with their lid. Reduce the heat and steam for 10 minutes. Lift the baskets from the pan with oven gloves. Put them on a large plate or dish and bring to the table, using bamboo tongs to serve.

Serve with green meadow sauce (p. 135) and *taramaroussia* (p. 55) in separate dishes. The combination of pink and green sauces with the white and green vegetables, is most appetising.

◦~∞~◦

STEAMED CABBAGE PARCELS

In this recipe, cabbage leaves are wrapped around a filling to make little parcels which are secured with string. They look very tempting. Bring the parcels directly to the table in the bamboo steaming baskets and hand scissors around the table to cut off the string when the parcels are served. The parcels are Chinese in style, as part of the filling includes cashew nuts, fresh ginger and soy sauce.

60 g/2 oz cashew nuts coarsely chopped	60 g/2 oz raisins
1 medium-sized cabbage	2-cm/1-inch piece fresh ginger, peeled and finely chopped
1 tablespoon peanut oil	1 egg, lightly beaten
1 garlic clove, unpeeled and lightly crushed	nutmeg
1 tablespoon soy sauce	salt
125 g/4 oz smoked tongue in 1 piece	freshly ground pepper
	12 pieces of string, each 30 cm/12 inches

On a baking tray, toast the cashew nuts for 20 minutes in a moderate oven, checking that they brown evenly. Reserve.

Take about 12 of the outer leaves from the cabbage. Wash them and steam them for 2 minutes. Refresh under cold water. Cut out most of the hard centre stem. Drain on a clean cloth, rough side down.

Chop about 125 g/4 oz of the cabbage heart (reserving the rest for another use). Heat the oil in a pan, add the garlic clove, fry it for a few seconds, and discard. Now sauté briefly the chopped cabbage. Remove from the heat and season with the soy sauce, salt and pepper. Reserve.

Cut the smoked tongue in small cubes and put it in a bowl with the cabbage heart, cashew nuts, raisins and ginger. Bind with the egg. Season with nutmeg, salt and pepper.

Put a little of the filling in the centre of one cabbage leaf and roll from stem end to top. Fold the sides over and tie with a piece of string. Repeat the operation until all the leaves are used. Fill three 15-cm/6-inch baskets with the parcels and set over a pan of boiling water. Cover with the bamboo lid and steam for 20–25 minutes. With oven gloves on, remove the baskets and put them, still stacked, on a plate or tray and serve.

STEAMED SWISS CHARD

Swiss chard, like spinach beet, is a type of beet or *Beta vulgaris*. It is grown not only for its large, curly, spinach-like leaves, but also for its ribbed white stems; it is indeed two vegetables in one. The white ribs are best steamed and made into a gratin. The dark green leaves with white veins are particularly suitable for wrapping, parcel-like, around sole fillets steamed in bamboo baskets. They can also be used for the recipe of smoked oysters steamed in vine leaves (p.64).

In this recipe, which uses the leaves only, the chard is prepared in a simple, but delectable manner. The few drops of lemon added at the end make all the difference.

I kg/2 lb Swiss chard	salt and freshly ground pepper
2 tablespoons olive oil	I lemon, cut in wedges
nutmeg	

Cut off the white stems and keep them to use in another recipe. Wash the leaves in plenty of water. Gather the chard in a neat bunch and drain, but not too thoroughly. Pour the olive oil into a tall saucepan, just wide enough to take the bunch of chard upright. Put in the vegetables with water still clinging to the leaves. Cover and cook over medium heat for 10 minutes; check once or twice that the vegetables are not catching at the bottom of the pan.

When the chard is ready, it will have reduced a great deal. Transfer it to a serving dish, seasoning with freshly grated nutmeg, salt and pepper. Squeeze over a few drops of lemon juice and decorate with lemon wedges. Serve with *sauce laitière* (p. 138).

STEAMED MOULI WITH WATERCRESS MAYONNAISE

Mouli is a long, white root, sometimes called Japanese horseradish. The taste is not so pungent as that of radishes, but rather similar to turnips

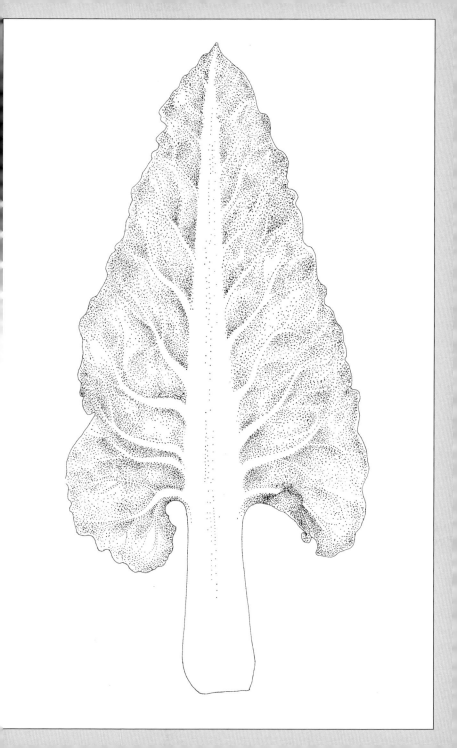

(by which it may be replaced in this recipe). Don't overcook the mouli or it will become stringy.

750 g/1 ½ lb mouli or turnips	salt and pepper

Peel and wash the mouli. Slice thinly and steam in a bamboo basket for 5–7 minutes. Serve in its basket with bamboo tongs instead of serving spoon and fork. Eat with this watercress mayonnaise.

WATERCRESS MAYONNAISE

1 bunch watercress, stems trimmed, chopped very fine	mustard
1 large egg at room temperature	about 150 ml/¼ pint peanut oil
1 teaspoon strong French	juice of ½ lemon
	salt and white pepper
	paprika

Break the egg into a food processor, add the mustard and blend. With the motor running, pour the oil in a stream through the funnel. Switch off and scrape the sides with a rubber spatula. Season and add the lemon juice. Rerun the motor for a few seconds, adding the watercress. Transfer the green mayonnaise to a pretty bowl, dusting with paprika. The use of the whole egg instead of two yolks, makes the mayonnaise lighter, rather more like a sauce.

SPROUT TOPS
WITH CACIOTTA CHEESE

In the markets in the south of France, they sell many different kinds of olives, some flavoured with herbs. The black ones flavoured with thyme and rosemary are my favourites, and I preserve them for use back in England after the holidays by covering them with olive oil in a glass jar. After a while the oil becomes even fruitier than before.

This is a recipe to use up the oil in which the olives have marinated.

Caciotta is a semi-soft white Italian cheese, very mild, with a texture between ricotta and mozzarella (but rather tastier than the latter). The sprout tops may be replaced by spring greens in this recipe with equal success.

125 g/4 oz caciotta cheese
2 tablespoons olive oil
salt and black pepper

500 g/1 lb sprout tops, end stems trimmed off, and washed

Cube the cheese in a little bowl and pour over the oil. Reserve. In a bamboo basket steam the sprout tops for 10–12 minutes. Meanwhile, warm a china salad bowl with boiling water. Pat it dry and put in the cheese and oil mixture. Transfer the vegetables from the steaming basket to the bowl. Season to taste and toss to coat with the dressing. Serve immediately.

FLAN DE COURGETTES

This is a very light course which can be eaten hot, lukewarm or cold. A brown or white earthenware pie dish looks pretty with wedges of the flan showing their mixture of green and yellow. I serve it with the burghul and yogurt salad (p. 43) or the multicoloured salad (p. 121).

FOR A 25-CM/10-INCH PIE DISH

4 medium-sized courgettes
nutmeg
pepper
salt
4 eggs

1 tablespoon cream
a sprig of fresh tarragon or parsley
125 g/4 oz Emmenthal or Gruyère

Top and tail the courgettes and slice thinly. Steam them for 3 minutes, or parboil for the same time. Refresh under the cold tap and let them drain. Pat dry with a kitchen towel. Season with 1 or 2 gratings of nutmeg, pepper and rather more salt. Arrange at the bottom of the buttered earthenware dish. In a small bowl, beat together the eggs, cream and chopped tarragon or parsley. Season to taste. Pour this mixture over the courgettes. Sprinkle over the grated cheese. Bake in the oven at gas 2/300°F/150°C for 45–50 minutes or until a golden crust has formed on the top.

SOUFFLÉ ROULÉ AUX ÉPINARDS

This delicious soufflé looks beautiful when the long green roll with pink stripes is brought to the table. The white creamy filling concealed in the centre is revealed when each guest takes a slice.

The method may seem elaborate on reading, but in fact it is easy to make the soufflé successfully. It requires just a little care and attention to the instructions. The great advantage of this dish is that it can be made ahead of time, as much as a day in advance, and re-heated in the oven, wrapped in foil.

I use sour cream for the filling because it sets instead of running when heated. As a final decoration, I like to surround the serving dish with tiny cooked carrots and, if available, baby sweet corns.

750 g/1½ lb fresh spinach or
500 g/1 lb frozen leaf spinach
100 g/3 oz butter
75 g/2½ oz flour
150 ml/¼ pint hot milk
mace

nutmeg
salt and pepper
2 eggs, separated
2–3 thin slices smoked salmon,
cut in narrow strips

FOR THE FILLING

1 large or 2 small smoked trout
3 tablespoons sour cream

1 tablespoon grated horseradish

Pre-heat the oven to gas 6/400°F/200°C. Wash the fresh spinach thoroughly and drain, but not completely, leaving a little water clinging to the leaves. In a saucepan, cook without extra water for 5 minutes, stirring with a wooden spoon until wilted and rather dry. Alternatively, chop the thawed spinach, squeezing out the water. Make a white sauce with the butter, flour and hot milk. Season to taste, being generous with the mace and nutmeg. Add the spinach and the 2 egg yolks. Whisk the egg whites until stiff. Fold into the spinach mixture carefully.

Take a baking tray (Swiss roll type is best) about 30 x 40 cm/ 12 x 16 inches and line it with foil, generously greased (this is important as otherwise the soufflé will stick). Spread the mixture evenly, and bake for 20 minutes in the preheated oven.

Meanwhile, prepare the filling: remove the skin and bones from the trout and flake the flesh into a bowl. Stir in the cream and horseradish. Reserve.

Have ready a slightly wet cloth and turn the soufflé onto it. Carefully peel off the foil. Trim the edges neatly. Now spread the filling lengthways down the centre and fold first one side and then the other over the middle so that the roll is the same length as the original soufflé but a third of the width. Place a new piece of buttered foil on top of the roll and turn it upside down. Now slide a baking tray underneath to carry it more easily and remove the cloth. Decorate the soufflé with the thin strips of smoked salmon, making a striped pattern. Wrap tightly in the foil and leave to rest for at least 2 hours (this allows the roll to keep its shape). Up to this stage the recipe can be prepared ahead of time and kept refrigerated until needed.

Re-heat the roll, still wrapped to keep it moist, in a moderate oven for 20 minutes. Remove the foil and transfer to an oblong dish (I use a china cake tray) and serve.

VARIATION

For the filling, use 250 g/8 oz chopped ham and 3 tablespoons sour cream. Decorate with 3 slices of ham cut in long strips.

CAVIAR D' AUBERGINES

At home we used to call this dish '*le caviar du pauvre*'. Serve this cream lukewarm to bring out the combined flavours of the cumin and the fruity olive oil. The yogurt prevents it being heavy. Eat with bread, or as a sauce with tomatoes.

2 large aubergines
6 tablespoons virgin olive oil
125 ml/¼ pint plain yogurt
1 tablespoon fresh dill or flat parsley, chopped

a pinch of ground cumin
1 small garlic clove (optional)
salt and pepper

Put the whole aubergines on a baking tray and bake in the oven at gas 5/375°F/190°C for 30–40 minutes or until the skin is dry and wrinkled, and the flesh feels soft when pressed. With a sharp knife, slit the skin lengthways and spoon out the hot flesh into a food processor or a blender. Blend until smooth and while the motor is running, pour in the olive oil in a thin stream. This will emulsify the aubergine purée like a mayonnaise. Transfer to a mixing bowl and add all the other ingredients. Check the seasoning. Keep covered at room temperature until required.

AUBERGINES CONFITES

After marinating for a month, the aubergines have a smooth and tender texture. Serve them as a starter with crisp toast, or as a side dish with cold meat.

FOR 3 JARS OF 500 ML/1 PINT EACH

1½ kg/3½ lb aubergines
salt
500 ml/1 pint water
250 ml/½ pint wine vinegar

3 garlic cloves, peeled
6 cardamom pods
olive oil

Wash the aubergines, trim, pat dry and cut them, unpeeled, into medium-sized slices. Lay them on an earthenware dish. Sprinkle each layer of aubergine with salt. Leave them to render their juices for 4–5 hours, then drain them.

Bring the water and vinegar to the boil. Poach the aubergine slices in small batches, letting them simmer for about 4 minutes. Drain and dry very thoroughly with a clean cloth or kitchen paper.

Place in preserving jars with the garlic cloves and the cardamom seeds. Pour over enough olive oil to reach the top. Secure tightly and leave to mature for at least a month.

BOHÉMIENNE EN CHARLOTTE

This is my adaptation of a French recipe which is normally made with eggs and cream. This version is lighter and will keep its shape in spite of the omission of setting ingredients.

Make this charlotte in summer, when the vegetables are at their best. I like to serve it sometimes with a sauce made of beaten yogurt, shredded fresh mint leaves, salt and pepper.

If the charlotte is to be kept in the refrigerator for more than a day, it is advisable to use an ovenproof glass dish, or to line the mould with foil. If you only decide after cooking to keep it longer than a day, let the charlotte get quite cold and then turn it out onto a plate, carefully wrap in cling-film and put back in the metal mould.

4 medium-sized aubergines	12 oz/350 g ricotta cheese
500 g/1 lb small courgettes	140 ml/¼ pint yogurt
a little thyme	about 1 glass of olive oil
4 firm tomatoes	salt and pepper
1 clove of garlic	

Wipe the aubergines and trim the stalks. Cut in fairly thin slices. Put them in a colander, sprinkling each layer with salt. Leave to drain for 1 hour. Rinse under cold water and pat dry.

Wipe and trim the courgettes. Cut in medium-sized slices. Heat 1 tablespoon of olive oil in a frying pan or a wok and sauté the courgettes briefly over a fierce heat until quite brown on both sides, but still underdone inside. That will take about 3 minutes. Season with the thyme, salt and pepper. Reserve.

Scald the tomatoes in boiling water for 1 minute. Peel them and cut into big chunks. Peel the garlic clove, split in two, discard the little green shoot and chop very fine. Heat 1 tablespoon of olive oil in a frying pan and sauté the garlic for 1 minute. Add the tomatoes, season and cook over a medium heat until they are mushy and most of the liquid has evaporated. Reserve.

Heat 2 tablespoons of oil in a sauté pan and brown a batch of aubergine slices on both sides. Don't overcrowd the pan. They will absorb a lot of oil so when you turn them press gently to extract a little of the oil. Repeat the operation until all the aubergine slices are done, using more oil when necessary.

In a small bowl beat together the ricotta and the yogurt. Season.

Pre-heat the oven to gas 4/350°F/180°C. Grease generously a charlotte mould 16 x 9 cm/6 x 3½ inches and line if necessary. Arrange a layer of overlapping aubergine slices in the bottom and around the sides of the mould. Spread with a little of the tomato mixture. Add a layer of courgette slices. Then top with some of the cheese mixture. Continue the layers finishing with aubergines. Cover tightly with foil and bake for 50 minutes.

Leave to cool for at least 2 hours and turn out onto a serving dish at the very last minute, as some of the juice will escape from the charlotte. You may decorate with half-slices of tomato all around. Serve cold or at room temperature.

PETITS POTS DE CAROTTES

This is a light summer dish which may be prepared in advance. I serve it in individual ramekins. I have some dark ochre ones from the

Dordogne, with a rough salt glaze finish; the carrot mixture looks very appetising in them. The *petits pots de carottes* can be served as a side dish for poultry and game.

60 g/2 oz almonds, skin removed	1 tablespoon fresh dill (or 1 teaspoon dried dill weed)
250 g/8 oz young carrots	2 tablespoons best quality
250 g/8 oz ricotta cheese	peanut oil
2 slices ham, chopped	salt and pepper

In a food processor, chop coarsely the peeled almonds. Reserve. Now chop finely the scrubbed carrots, turning the motor on and off to ensure that they are evenly chopped. In a bowl, break the ricotta with a wooden spoon, add the other ingredients until well amalgamated. Check the seasoning. Press down into the little ramekins. They may be served refrigerated or at room temperature with hot pitta bread and butter.

SOUFFLÉ IN GLOBE ARTICHOKES

As they cook, the artichokes impart their flavour to the soufflé mixture, giving it a most delicate taste. Use the outer leaves to scoop out the soufflé.

6 globe artichokes (large Breton type are best)	350 g/12 oz grated Gruyère or farmhouse Cheddar
125 g/4 oz butter	a little parsley, the flat sort
125 g/4 oz flour	preferably
1 generous 500 ml/pint rich milk	salt
	pepper
5 eggs, separated	nutmeg

Cut the top leaves of each artichoke with a sharp knife. Have ready a large pan three-quarters filled with salted, acidulated boiling water. Cook them, covered, for about 20 minutes. Drain upside down in order to get out as much liquid as possible. Pull out the centre leaves and the choke, using a small silver spoon to scoop out all the little bits. This operation will leave a nest to be filled with the soufflé mixture.

Pre-heat the oven to gas 7/425°F/220°C. Make a very thick béchamel sauce with the butter, flour and milk. When cooled, add the egg yolks, grated cheese (reserving 2 tablespoons for the top), chopped parsley and seasoning, being generous with the nutmeg. Beat the egg whites until quite firm. Fold a cupful into the sauce to lighten it, and then fold in the rest, taking care not to deflate the whites. Spoon some of the soufflé mixture inside each artichoke. Dot with a little butter and the remaining cheese. Bake for 45–50 minutes.

MARROW CUPS
WITH SCRAMBLED EGGS

The marrow is cut in large, cup-like slices and filled with scrambled eggs and watercress. The marrow flesh, when cooked, becomes a light green, slightly translucent, which makes a delicate blend of colours with the watercress in the centre. I like this dish with the tomato ice (p. 90) and the *tarte aux pommes d'Agnès* (p. 164).

1–1½ kg/2–2½ lb marrow	1 tablespoon chopped mint
6 large eggs	mace
1 tablespoon cream	1 tablespoon butter
1 teaspoon water	2 bunches watercress
3 tablespoons chopped parsley	salt and pepper
1 tablespoon chopped tarragon	

Peel the marrow and cut in 6 slices. With a small spoon, scoop out and discard the seeds and woolly flesh in the centre. Steam the slices for about 15 minutes or until the flesh is soft but not floppy when pierced with a skewer. Season. Leave to cool and place on a flat dish.

In a small bowl, beat together the eggs, cream, water, parsley, tarragon, mint and a little mace. Season to taste. In a heavy saucepan, melt the butter and cook the eggs, stirring constantly: they should be scrambled to a soft consistency. Remember that they continue to cook off the heat, so watch them carefully. Cool on a plate.

Trim and discard hard stems from the watercress. Steam for 3 minutes. Chop coarsely on a wooden board. Season with salt and pepper. Fill the marrow cups with the egg mixture. Then heap a little of the watercress on the top.

VARIATION
Fill the marrow cups with the mixture from the recipe for *petits pots de carottes* on page 104.

TURNIP PURÉE WITH PINE NUTS

I choose rather small turnips, as large ones tend to be fibrous. The potato will give body to the purée which is otherwise too watery. The resin-like flavour of the pine nuts is enhanced when they are lightly toasted.

2 tablespoons pine nuts
500 g/1 lb turnips
1 sprig fresh sage
1 medium-sized potato, peeled
and cooked

1 tablespoon double cream
1 tablespoon butter
salt and white pepper

Lightly toast the pine nuts in a moderate oven. They will take about 10 minutes. Peel and quarter the turnips. Cook them in salted, boiling water with the sage sprigs for about 20 minutes, or until soft when pierced with a skewer. Drain and discard the sage. Purée with the peeled, cooked potato, using the finest mesh of a vegetable mouli, or a food processor. Stir in the cream and butter and season to taste. Transfer to an ovenproof serving dish. Cover with foil and keep in a warm oven until needed. Just before serving, scatter over the pine nuts.

FLUFFY PARSNIPS

In France, parsnips are considered good only for cattle feed, not human consumption. They bring back memories of the war. I find it very sad that this winter root vegetable is so neglected, as it can be prepared in many delicious ways. My recipe is a very light version of a purée. To achieve the right fluffiness you need a food processor.

3 medium-sized parsnips
1 egg
1 teaspoon Barbados sugar (the
very dark sort)
a few shavings of nutmeg

pepper
salt
1 walnut-sized piece of butter
4 thin bacon slices, fried and
broken in small bits

Peel the parsnips, removing all the blackened parts, and cut into big chunks. Have ready some salted, boiling water and cook the vegetables for about 20 minutes or until they are very soft when tested with a skewer. In the food processor, whizz the whole egg for a few seconds. Stop the machine and add the drained parsnips and the sugar. Process for 2 minutes. Season to taste and put in the piece of butter. Run the motor again, the purée will fluff and expand and look light like a kind of soufflé. Transfer to a serving dish. Sprinkle with the bacon bits. The crispy bacon contrasts nicely with the smooth parsnips.

YAMS WITH SOUR CREAM

Yams can now be bought quite easily from good green-grocers. The ones we find here are normally grown in Spain (Malaga pink). They have a terracotta-coloured skin with bright orange flesh. In size and shape they are similar to potatoes, and they can be treated like potatoes, though the flesh is sweeter and the skin has an after-taste not unlike mango. In America, they are part of the traditional Thanksgiving meal, along with turkey and cranberry sauce.

2–3 medium-sized yams, each weighing about 300 g/10 oz	pinch of cinnamon
150 ml/¼ pint sour cream	pinch of brown sugar
a little dill, preferably fresh	salt
	freshly ground pepper

Wash the yams under cold water, but don't scrub them as they would bleed and the flesh lose all its colour. Bake in their skins at gas 4/350°F/180°C for 1 hour or until done. Leave them to cool completely so that the flesh becomes firm and waxy. Slit the wrinkled skin and peel off (I keep the skin to eat later, seasoned with salt and pepper, with a little butter sandwiched inside.) You are now left with the beautiful orange flesh, which you slice thinly. Arrange the slices, overlapping them on a serving dish of a contrasting colour. Salt a little.

For the sauce, mix all the other ingredients together, season with salt and pepper and pour over the centre of the yams, making a long white stripe. Decorate with dill plumes if you can find any fresh, or otherwise sprinkle a little dried dill on the top.

BOUBOU POTATOES

The potatoes should be of a waxy variety such as Désirée. Try to choose ones that are flattish like pebbles. During cooking, their cut side forms a new golden skin which puffs up. When they are on your plate, you split the crusty top and insert a piece of salty butter.

There is nothing glamorous about this dish, but one can easily become addicted to it. I serve boubou potatoes with walnut and basil sauce (p. 136), a green salad and an assortment of cheeses, all brought to the table at the same time.

12 waxy potatoes of even, medium size	sea salt butter

Pre-heat the oven to gas 8/450°F/230°C. Halve the clean, unpeeled potatoes lengthways. Sprinkle some sea salt on the cut side. Put cut side up on a tray placed on the top shelf of the oven. Cook until done (the time depends on the size of the potatoes but it should be about 15 minutes). Serve with fresh butter.

ALIGOT À MA FAÇON

This is a dish from the Auvergne, one of my favourite parts of central France. There it was traditionally eaten on Fridays when one could not eat meat, and, as the sea was so far away, fish was hard to come by. The cheese used in the Auvergne is fresh Cantal, which has a milder, smokier taste than the Cheddar I have suggested below; but I find that mixed with ricotta the taste of this version is good, and the dish, though an earthy one, is slightly lighter.

The *aligot* should ideally be made in a heavy saucepan that can be brought to the table and set on a hot plate like fondue, so that everyone can scoop out the threads of golden purée.

1 kg/2 lb floury potatoes	250 g/8 oz mild Cheddar, cubed
salt	250 g/8 oz ricotta or
white pepper	mascarpone cheese, cubed
grating of nutmeg	small garlic clove
60 g/2 oz salty butter	

Boil the potatoes in their skins for 20 minutes. Drain, peel and purée them. Season with salt, pepper and nutmeg. Put the purée in a heavy saucepan, add the butter and heat, mixing well with a wooden spatula until the butter is melted. Take off the heat and little by little add the cubed cheeses and crushed garlic, lifting the mass from underneath as you go. The *aligot* will make long strands which you keep on pulling. Put back on the heat once or twice to keep it warm, but do not overheat or the mixture will become grainy. Serve at once.

As it is quite a substantial dish, serve with a green salad or steamed Swiss chard (p. 96).

VEGETABLE COUSCOUS

Couscous, available from middle-eastern stores, is a semolina made from hard wheat grain and is a speciality of the Maghreb countries (Morocco, Tunisia, Algeria). It usually comes in 3 different sizes; I think medium is best. You can also buy a pre-cooked couscous from most supermarkets which takes about half the usual steaming time. Read the instructions on the packet.

Couscous is normally steamed over a tall pan (*couscoussière*) of boiling broth in which fowl, meat and vegetables are cooked. I use a large Chinese bamboo basket lined with muslin, but a sieve would be adequate. The important thing is to make sure that the couscous container fits tightly over the pan used. Couscous is very easy to prepare; the only thing to remember is to keep it free of lumps.

I use very large, plump, Lexia or Malaga raisins; their flavour is quite different from that of the ordinary sort sold coated with mineral oil.

Serve with *aubergines confites* (p. 102).

250 g/8 oz couscous	500 g/1 lb pumpkin or swede
250 ml/½ pint tepid, slightly salted water	125 g/4 oz butter
	100 g/3 oz whole almonds, skinned, split in two
1 litre/2 pints vegetable or chicken stock	500 g/1 lb leeks, cleaned, cut in 2-cm/1-inch slices
cumin	100 g/3 oz raisins
saffron	250 g/8 oz cooked chick-peas
cayenne pepper	3 tablespoons fruity olive oil
salt	

Spread the couscous on a metal tray and sprinkle over half of the salted water. Leave for 20 minutes in order to let it absorb the water, then separate the grains with your fingers. Repeat the operation. After a further 20 minutes, separate the grains again.

In a large pan, bring the stock to the boil. Spice and salt to your taste. Put in the pumpkin or swede, peeled and cut into big chunks. Put the couscous in a bamboo basket lined with damp muslin, and set over the pan. Steam, uncovered, for about 40 minutes. From time to time, rake with a fork to make sure that there are no lumps.

When the couscous has been cooking for 20 minutes, add to the basket the sliced leeks, raisins and chick-peas. Steam, covered, for a further 20 minutes.

Meanwhile, in a small frying pan, melt 1 tablespoon of the butter and sauté the split almonds until a light golden colour and reserve.

Transfer the contents of the couscous basket to a large plate and toss in the remaining butter and olive oil. Pile in the centre of a large, serving dish. Surround by the drained swede or pumpkin pieces, and stud here and there with the almonds. Serve with a jugful of the spicy broth.

Left-over couscous is very good served cold with more olive oil and a generous handful of chopped parsley added to it.

MALFATI

These are green gnocchi made with parsley instead of spinach. They are very delicate and really don't need any sauce, which might be overpowering. I prefer them with melted butter and plenty of grated cheese. A blend of Parmesan and Emmenthal is a good combination. Any left-overs are delicious eaten cold with olive oil, or re-heated in steaming baskets. *Malfati* are prepared in two stages which makes them a good choice for a dinner party.

250 g/8 oz ricotta cheese	salt
350 g/12 oz parsley, finely chopped	pepper
2 egg whites	about 125 g/4 oz melted butter
1 heaped tablespoon flour	100 g/3 oz Parmesan
	100 g/3 oz Emmenthal

In a large bowl, crumble the ricotta, blend in the washed, finely chopped parsley, the egg whites and the sieved flour. Season with salt and pepper. Leave the mixture to rest for several hours or, even better, overnight. (This will allow it to dry out a little, which makes it easier to handle.)

Flour a board and your hands and shape the *malfati* mixture into little croquettes the size of a cork, and roll them in flour. Avoid putting them on the top of each other, or they might stick together. Have ready a large pan filled with gently boiling, salted water. Poach the *malfati* in batches; when they rise to the surface, lift out and drain. Place them in a buttered ovenproof dish and coat with the melted butter. Repeat the operation until the *malfati* are all done, keeping the dish, covered, in a warm oven. Raise the heat 10 minutes before serving, and serve with more melted butter and plenty of grated cheese.

RED AND YELLOW
TAGLIATELLE PRIMAVERA

This is a pasta dish which is good warm and even better eaten cold as a salad. It is very suitable for a buffet party. All the spring vegetables are barely cooked and give a crunchy bite to the pasta. You will find that the difference in taste is well worth the trouble of making your own tagliatelle.

The red peppercorns I have suggested in the ingredients (*Schinus molle, baies roses*) have a taste which is, I would say, a cross between green peppercorns and juniper berries. They are milder than the former and more fragrant than the latter. They are quite difficult to get, but good delicatessens stock them.

FOR ABOUT 10 PEOPLE

250 g/8 oz fresh red tagliatelle	250 g/8 oz small French beans
250 g/8 oz fresh yellow tagliatelle	250 g/8 oz baby courgettes (yellow kind, if available)
125 ml/¼ pint walnut oil, or half sunflower oil, half walnut oil	3 tablespoons chopped parsley
250 g/8 oz broccoli	10 red peppercorns (optional)
250 g/8 oz mange-tout peas, topped and tailed	salt and freshly ground pepper

To make red tagliatelle, follow the recipe for green pasta, but replace the spinach with 2 tablespoons of tomato paste.

Bring to the boil a large pan filled with water. Add 1 tablespoon of salt and 1 tablespoon of oil. Put in the tagliatelle (red and yellow at the same time) and cook for about 3 to 4 minutes; they should be *al dente*. Drain. Put in a bowl and toss in the oil. Adjust the seasoning. Reserve.

Using 2 bamboo steamers (method p. 92), first steam the broccoli for 5 minutes; add the mange-tout peas, French beans and the sliced (but not peeled) courgettes and steam for a further 5 minutes. Remove the baskets and refresh the vegetables, still in the baskets, under cold running water. They should be underdone.

Slice the broccoli stalks and separate the florets. Break the French beans in two. Put all the vegetables and the parsley in the pasta bowl, season and mix well. Transfer to a serving dish and decorate with lightly crushed red peppercorns.

If you use bought pasta for this dish try the spiral kind called fusilli. They have a pretty shape and they retain more of the dressing in their curls.

SWEET BASIL SANDWICH

'For cruel 'tis,' said she,
'To steal my basil-pot away from me.'
John Keats, *Isabella; or, The Pot of Basil*

Basil is a name derived from the Greek word for king. Its aroma is as complex as a perfume. You can grow it indoors: the plant will need repotting once towards the end of July and will keep on growing happily until early autumn. Pinch out the new shoots at the top to make it bushier. The leaves are so fragrant that touching them slightly in passing fills the room with their sweet and peppery aroma.

Basil has a great affinity with tomatoes; it can also be used to make the Italian pesto sauce. A tablespoon of pesto will enhance a mayonnaise or a plain dressing. I remember some friends in the country giving me olive oil in which sweet basil had been steeped; it was a real treat, poured in a stream over cold pasta or thinly sliced ricotta cheese.

Make some sandwiches with wholemeal bread (preferably home-made – see p. 39), cream cheese or mascarpone cheese, tomatoes, walnut halves and torn basil leaves (do not cut them or they will lose some of their pungency), salt and freshly ground pepper. Eat slowly, savouring each mouthful.

SALADS

SORREL AND POMEGRANATE SALAD

In autumn, when pomegranates are in full season, I like to sprinkle a green salad with their garnet-like, shiny, round seeds. They burst into sweet and sour juice when eaten. I am fascinated by the intricate design which appears when you cut the fruit in section. The seeds freeze very well and I keep little bags of them (handful-size) to use when required.

Sorrel grows like a weed and needs no care. I wonder why it is so difficult to get it from greengrocers. It is easy to grow in a garden, and I grow it successfully on my balcony so I can pull off a few leaves to add pungency to a salad.

I bunch of sorrel leaves	4–5 tablespoons emulsified
I Webb's lettuce	vinaigrette (p. 134)
½ pomegranate	salt
	pepper

Cut the stalks off the sorrel leaves. Wash, dry and cut with scissors into strips. Cut the lettuce in sections, like an orange. Discard the white membrane from the pomegranate and pull out the seeds. (Freeze the seeds from the other half of the fruit and use for decorating a fruit salad.) In a salad bowl, toss the lettuce sections and strips of sorrel with the vinaigrette. Season, then scatter the pomegranate seeds over the salad to decorate, and serve immediately.

WATERCRESS AND ORANGE SALAD

The deep green of the watercress contrasts dramatically with the sun-like orange slices. The peppery tang of the leaves and the sweet-and-sour taste of the fruit combine to make this salad very refreshing. It would be ideal with a rich winter meal. Choose watercress with large leaves.

I serve most of the stalks of the watercress, which are crunchy. If they are too long, chop them into small pieces. Cider vinegar, which is milder than wine, is preferable for this salad.

2 bunches watercress   2 small oranges

DRESSING

1 tablespoon cider vinegar   freshly ground pepper
4–5 tablespoons light oil   salt
   (sunflower preferably)

Prepare the dressing. Trim the watercress stalks. Put the sprigs in a bowl and toss in half of the dressing. Peel, slice and remove the pips from the oranges.

Put nearly all the watercress in a crown-like ring around the outer edge of a wide, shallow serving dish. Arrange the orange slices, slightly overlapping, and fill the centre with the remaining watercress. Spoon the rest of the dressing over the oranges. Serve without refrigerating.

SPECTRUM SALAD

This bright salad makes a change from the usual austere green salad. It demands effort as the ingredients have to be searched for, but it is worthwhile if you are a salad addict as I am. The reward at the end is twofold: the combination of tastes and colours.

A hint that I found in an old Yorkshire Women's Institute recipe book is to put a piece of coal in the water in which salad (or a vegetable) is washed. It will miraculously revive even the most withered leaves.

The purple cauliflower listed below is not the purple-sprouting broccoli, although it is very similar in taste. The sort I mean is one large head, about the size of a small white cauliflower. Only the deep purple florets are used in this recipe. (The stalks may be sautéed and replace the spring greens in the yellow pancakes recipe p.47)

In general, I don't like tinned food, but whole baby corn is one of the few exceptions. They are sweet and delicious and about the size of your little finger. You will find them in Chinese supermarkets.

As a foreigner, I have frequently been confused about names given to salads and vegetables. But perhaps I am not alone in feeling that a few descriptions would be useful to clear up some of the confusion. Below are the botanical names and some of the more commonly found foreign names for unusual or old-fashioned salad ingredients.

CORN SALAD
Lamb's lettuce
Valerianella locusta
Mâche (French)

Grows in little clusters of dark green leaves shaped like lambs' tongues. In France, mixed with beetroot, it is a very popular winter salad. Corn salad has a mild, sweetish taste.

ROCKET
Eruca sativa
Roquette (French)
Rucola (Italian)
Arugula (U.S.)

In Italy, rocket is still much used to flavour salad, and in the south of France it is one of the ingredients of the much appreciated Mesclun salad. Rocket's taste is peppery and clean at the same time.

RED CHICORY
*Chichorium intybus Endive de
   Trévise (French)*
Rossa di Treviso (Italian)

Red chicory is incorrectly called radicchio by greengrocers in England. It belongs to the Belgian chicory family and looks like a small cabbage, but with a beautiful deep crimson colour, streaked with white. It has a slightly bitter taste.

500 g/1 lb corn salad
250 g/8 oz rocket
2 red chicory heads

1 tin whole baby corn (or pack of fresh)

DRESSING

1 tablespoon tarragon vinegar
   5 tablespoons peanut oil

salt and freshly ground pepper

First prepare the dressing, mixing all the ingredients together. Detach the leaves from the little bunches of corn salad. Wash very thoroughly in several changes of water. Drain. Wash the rocket leaves and dry well. Remove the red chicory leaves from the stems, wash and dry. Cut off most of the stem from the purple cauliflower and break into little florets.

Toss all the salad ingredients with the vinaigrette in a large, shallow bowl and serve.

SCARLET SALAD

Serve this salad in a bowl of a contrasting colour (for example, green or white) to achieve a dramatic effect.

1 bunch of small radishes	1 medium-sized red chicory
2 medium-sized cooked beetroots	3 small tomatoes

DRESSING

4–5 tablespoons emulsified vinaigrette (p. 134)	1 teaspoon dill weed
1 dessertspoonful grated horseradish	salt, pepper

Quarter the radishes (or slice them if they are long ones). Slice the peeled beetroots then cut each slice in long sticks. Tear the leaves of the red chicory into bite-sized pieces. Peel the tomatoes (first steeping them in boiling water for 1 minute) and quarter them.

Toss everything together with the dressing.

MULTICOLOURED SALAD

This salad is simple, but looks spectacular, more like a still life painting of the Fauvist school. A beautiful array of colours is mingled together: the small, round, yellow and large, uneven, red tomatoes; the mauve chive flowers; the shiny, plump, black olives; the green mint leaves and the white mozzarella.

2 large red tomatoes
4 yellow tomatoes
1 mozzarella cheese
2 sprigs of fresh mint
2–3 chive flowers

about 15 black Italian olives
salt
freshly ground pepper
5 tablespoons fruity olive oil

Scald the red tomatoes in boiling water for 1 minute and peel. Slice across, not down, to show the beauty of the pattern. Slice the yellow tomatoes, but do not peel them, as under the bright skin the flesh is pallid. Cut the mozzarella fairly thin. Pull the mint leaves from their stalks.

Now take a large, flat dish of a bright colour, preferably green or blue. Arrange alternate, slightly overlapping slices of tomatoes and cheese. Tuck whole mint leaves here and there. Scatter petals of the chive flowers all over. Stud with the black olives. Season generously with salt and pepper. Lastly dribble over the olive oil, making sure to coat all the salad. Serve to artistically-inclined friends.

SPINACH AND STILTON SALAD

If you have a garden, you will be able to pick young, tender spinach leaves, which go well with sesame seeds toasted to a light brown in a moderate oven for about 20 minutes. When they are toasted, they give a bacon-like taste to the food to which they are added. Roquefort cheese can be used instead of Stilton.

500 g/1 lb young spinach
1 tablespoon toasted sesame
seeds

60 g/2 oz Stilton
1 marigold flower

DRESSING

1 teaspoon French mustard
2 teaspoons tarragon vinegar

3–4 tablespoons oil (peanut
preferably)
salt, pepper

Remove the spinach stems, wash the leaves scrupulously in cold water several times and drain well. Slice them in 2-cm/1-inch pieces. Toss in the vinaigrette and sprinkle over the toasted sesame seeds. They will cling to the leaves and give a speckled effect. Add the crumbled Stilton and marigold petals.

PARSLEY SALAD

Some week-ends I stay with friends in the country whose kitchen garden is bordered by rows of parsley. I feel no embarrassment at bringing back bagfuls of it and I use it instead of spinach for home-made green pasta or *malfati* (p. 113) or making lemon and parsley ice, a Victorian favourite.

I have found that parsley is invigorating, and treat it more like a vegetable in its own right than as a herb to be used sparingly. You can make a parsley salad with vinaigrette, but I prefer yogurt and lemon because they don't interfere with the clean taste of the parsley.

250 g/8 oz parsley	salt
250 ml/½ pint yogurt	freshly ground pepper
juice of 1 lemon	

Clean the parsley very thoroughly, changing the water several times if necessary. Drain well and leave to dry for a while. Chop the parsley, but not too fine, using a little of the stalks as they are very fragrant. Blend the yogurt and lemon juice together. Stir in the parsley. Season to taste. Serve very cold.

COURGETTE AND WALNUT SALAD

It is quite surprising how courgettes, served cold, make a delicious salad, and toasted walnuts bring a new dimension to this dish. I like to serve it in summer with *bacalhau-braz* (p. 61) and an orange salad (p. 146) to end the meal.

100 g/3 oz walnut halves	1 tablespoon tarragon vinegar
4 medium-sized courgettes	1 teaspoon dried tarragon
a few borage flowers	salt
DRESSING	white pepper
1 teaspoon French mustard	5–6 tablespoons walnut oil

Toast the walnut halves in the oven (gas 5/375°F/190°C) for about 20 minutes. Meanwhile, blanch the sliced but not peeled courgettes, or steam them for 2–3 minutes. Refresh under the cold tap. They should be crisp and yet tender.

Now prepare the dressing as follows: in a small bowl mix together the mustard and the tarragon vinegar. In the palm of one hand, crush the dried tarragon with the thumb of the other hand and add to the mustard mixture. Leave for a few minutes. Season with salt and freshly ground white pepper, and gradually beat in the walnut oil, as you would for a mayonnaise. The dressing should look creamy. Toss the courgettes in it and add the cooled walnuts. Transfer to a serving dish and decorate with borage flowers.

LE GRAND SALLET

This salad was inspired after reading *The English hus-wife* by Gervase Markham (1615). Purslane (*Portulaca sativa*) is a sprawling plant with clusters of thick, fleshy leaves. It is still popular in Mediterranean countries and though now neglected in England, it was common in Elizabethan times. I buy it from Greek greengrocers who always sell it during the summer months.

This sallet is quite a substantial dish and could be the centre-piece of a light supper. The apricots may be replaced by dried figs.

a few sprigs of purslane
3 heads of chicory
about 6–8 radishes or capers
60 g/2 oz dried apricots (or
dried figs)

60 g/2 oz blanched split
almonds
120 g/4 oz prawns, peeled and
deveined

DRESSING

125 ml/¼ pint double cream
3 tablespoons single cream
juice of ½ lemon
a pinch of dry mustard

a little cayenne pepper
salt
petals from a few chive flowers

In a small bowl, prepare the dressing, blending together all the ingredients. Check the seasoning.

Pull out the rosettes of leaves from the purslane sprigs. Cut the chicory into 1-cm/¹⁄₂-inch slices. Slice the radishes thinly. Shred the dried apricots (or dried figs). Put them all in a shallow china dish along with the split almonds and the prawns. Stir in the cream dressing. Dust with a little more cayenne pepper, the chive petals, and refrigerate until needed.

CELERY AND BANANA SALAD

This may seem an odd combination, but the blandness of the bananas balances the crunchiness of the celery well.

2 bananas, not too ripe
4–5 tablespoons double cream
1 teaspoon French mustard
salt
pepper

1 head celery, chopped fairly
small
a few Chinese cabbage leaves
1 teaspoon fennel seeds

Peel and slice the bananas. In a small bowl, blend the double cream and the mustard. Season. Put the celery and the banana in a large bowl and toss in the dressing. Adjust the seasoning if necessary and refrigerate.

Before serving, lay a few Chinese cabbage leaves on a pretty wicker tray and fill each one with a little of the salad, sprinkling over the fennel seeds.

GRAPE AND RADISH SALAD

Always look for small, firm radishes as the large ones tend to be hollow and too soft. If you grow your own radishes (buy seeds for the long variety), the leaves may be steamed and served as a vegetable or used for a soup. *Potage de fanes* is still served in the provinces of France.

1 large bunch radishes	500 g/1 lb black grapes
500 g/1 lb white grapes	

DRESSING

3 tablespoons yogurt	1 teaspoon French mustard
3 tablespoons sour cream	salt and pepper
a few sprigs of fresh dill or 2	
teaspoons dry dill weed	

Chop the dill coarsely if using fresh, and reserve one sprig. Mix all the other ingredients of the dressing.

Slice the radishes after trimming them. Halve the grapes lengthways, discarding any pips. Toss altogether with the dressing. Decorate with the reserved dill sprig and chill.

RHUBARB AND MINT SALAD

An unusual sweet-and-sour salad made with the first outdoor rhubarb in early April. The taste of fresh mint reminds you that spring is back.

500 g/1 lb very young rhubarb stems
1 tablespoon brown sugar

about 10 mint leaves
rosemary flowers

DRESSING

1 tablespoon sherry vinegar
5 tablespoons virgin olive oil

salt and freshly ground pepper

Cut the rhubarb in small pieces and put it in a serving dish. Sprinkle with brown sugar and marinate for about 1 hour.

Prepare the vinaigrette and pour over the rhubarb and sugar. Cut the mint leaves into long shreds and scatter, with the rosemary flowers, on the top of the salad just before serving.

CARROT AND ORANGE SALAD

This salad definitely has a taste of far away. Carrot and orange soup is so delicious that I thought of a salad using them both. It only seems to work, however, if you add ginger. Ginger gives a hotness somehow quite unexpected in a salad. Fresh roots only should be used, as the dried ones lose most of their sweet and scented flavour.

juice of 1 orange
1 small handful of currants
5 medium-sized carrots
2-cm/1-inch piece fresh ginger root

2–3 tablespoons olive oil
salt and pepper
1 knob of butter
1 tablespoon sesame seeds
2 tablespoons chopped parsley

Let the currants marinate in the orange juice. Meanwhile, peel the carrots and grate them with the coarse blade of a vegetable mouli, then place them in a bowl. Peel the ginger, shave it with a small, sharp knife, and chop in tiny bits. Add to the carrots. Make the dressing with the drained orange juice and the olive oil. Season and pour over the salad. Add the currants. Melt the butter in a small frying pan, and when it starts to bubble, add the sesame seeds. Watch them and shake the pan from time to time, as they tend to pop up and burn easily. (Don't forget that nuts and seeds keep on cooking even off the heat.)

Lay the salad on a shallow, white, oval dish and sprinkle with the sesame seeds and parsley. Serve.

RED BEAN SALAD IN PLUM SAUCE

This is a Russian salad originating from Georgia. I use tinned, plump Californian red kidney beans. The earthiness of the salad is lifted by the unusual combination of fresh coriander and basil.

1 garlic clove	1 tablespoon red wine vinegar
½ teaspoon salt	5 tablespoons damson jam
a dash of cayenne	1 tablespoon oil
6 basil leaves, chopped	350 g/12 oz cooked red kidney
a few sprigs of fresh coriander, chopped	beans, drained

Crush the garlic with the salt. Add the cayenne, basil and some of the coriander and mash the mixture to a smooth paste. Combine vinegar and jam in an enamelled or stainless steel pan and boil over high heat, stirring constantly, until the jam is dissolved. Rub the mixture through a fine sieve, add the oil, then gradually beat it into the garlic and herb paste. Add the beans and toss gently but thoroughly. Cover and refrigerate overnight. Serve decorated with the remaining coriander leaves.

RED CABBAGE AND JUNIPER SALAD

A winter salad which goes well with game. The juniper berries give a woody and slightly sweet taste to the dressing. The red cabbage imparts a pink tinge to the cream. If you have a few cooked chestnuts, they would be a nice addition to the salad.

½ medium-sized red cabbage   a little parsley

DRESSING

125 ml/¼ pint sour cream	paprika
3 tablespoons yogurt or	salt
buttermilk	freshly ground coarse pepper
6 juniper berries	a handful of currants

First make the dressing, to allow the juniper berries to develop their flavour in the cream. In a small bowl, beat the sour cream and the yogurt (or buttermilk) with a fork until smooth. In a mortar, crush the juniper with a pestle and blend into the dressing. Add the currants. Season to taste with salt, paprika and coarsely ground pepper.

Now shred the red cabbage very thinly with a sharp stainless steel knife, discarding the hard core at the bottom of the leaves. Separate the strands in a large, shallow salad bowl. Toss in the dressing. Last, decorate with the finely chopped parsley and the chestnuts, if used.

PEAR AND SMOKED CHICKEN SALAD

You can buy smoked chickens from most good butchers or fishmongers. They are moist and gamy-tasting, and have the advantage of keeping for months (the date limit is given on the packet). It is useful to keep a smoked chicken in the refrigerator in case of an impromptu meal. For this salad you will need only the breasts or thighs. The pear's sweetness goes well with the smoky taste of the chicken. One day I replaced the fresh pears by half the quantity of pickled ones and it worked beautifully.

2 ripe pears (Comice are best)	cayenne pepper
juice of ½ lemon	salt
2 tablespoons oil	1 bunch watercress
2 slices stale wholemeal bread	about ¼ smoked chicken, thinly
125 g/4 oz cottage cheese	sliced
about 10 walnut halves,	1 tablespoon chopped parsley
chopped coarsely	

Quarter, peel and core the pears, and cut them in chunks. Toss them with the lemon juice to avoid discolouring. Reserve. In a frying pan, heat the oil and fry the cubed bread on both sides. Drain on a paper towel. In a small bowl, beat the cottage cheese, blend in the walnuts and season with cayenne and salt.

Put the watercress in a layer at the bottom of a serving dish. Place on top the thin slices of chicken. Cover evenly with the pears. Coat with the cottage cheese mixture. Scatter the parsley on the top and lastly place at random the fried croûtons.

DRESSINGS
AND SAUCES

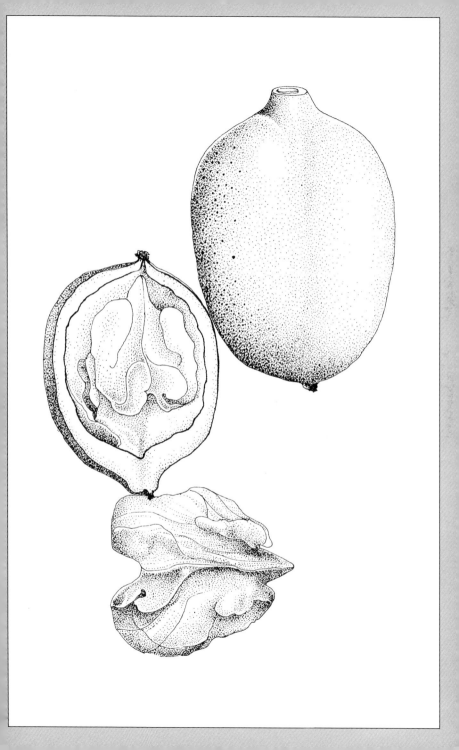

Sauces can be rich and elaborate, but that is not the aim of this chapter. Here you will find lighter sauces, which do not mask or overpower the dishes they accompany. These sauces do not detract from the natural flavour of food and this is especially important when they are to be served just with vegetables as is often the case here. The recipes are easy to follow and prepared in a matter of minutes. Though not nouvelle cuisine, these sauces and dressings are, I think, a little innovative. As they are prepared without fuss, they can be used for everyday meals and need not be reserved for special occasions.

MY SPECIAL VINAIGRETTE

What is as important as the method for this emulsified dressing is to have first class ingredients. There is little point in putting much effort into the preparation of a vinaigrette if the raw materials are not right: it will never taste good.

If you use dried herbs, always crush them with one thumb in the palm of your other hand to release the fragrant oil before adding to the vinaigrette.

1 teaspoon strong French mustard
freshly ground pepper
sea salt
1 tablespoon wine vinegar, red or white, but preferably flavoured, say, with tarragon

about 5 tablespoons olive oil, cold-pressed
1 tablespoon chopped fresh dill or tarragon, or 1 teaspoon dried

Put the mustard, pepper and a little salt in a small bowl. (I have a little sugar bowl with a rounded bottom which I use exclusively for this.) With a fork (this is essential), blend in the vinegar. Now, beating constantly with the fork, add the oil, first drop by drop, then in a stream. The vinaigrette is eventually emulsified like a mayonnaise. Add the herb and cover until required.

If you keep the dressing for a while it might separate, so beat again with a fork before using.

~~~

GREEN MEADOW SAUCE

I chose this name because I noticed that in France, meadows often lead to a stream where wild watercress grows. Of course, for this recipe it is the cultivated sort which is used.

This cold sauce is good eaten with salads, fish or eggs. If it is to be served with a hot dish, leave it at room temperature for an hour or so.

2 bunches watercress
1 bunch parsley
1 sprig fresh tarragon (or ½ tablespoon dried)
a few blades of chive (or ½ tablespoon dried)
juice of ½ lemon

4 tablespoons walnut oil
350 g/12 oz fromage blanc (p. 16)
1 teaspoon Worcestershire sauce
salt and white pepper

Chop together very finely the watercress, parsley, tarragon and chives. Add the lemon juice and walnut oil. Blend in the fromage blanc thoroughly. Season with Worcestershire sauce, salt and white pepper. Cover and refrigerate.

~~~

HORSERADISH AND DILL SAUCE

This sauce is one of the best companions for an assortment of smoked fish. It is simple and quickly made. The cream gives a sour tang which is the right taste with oily fish.

2 tablespoons grated horseradish
250 ml/½ pint sour cream
juice of ½ lemon
few drops Tabasco sauce

1 large sprig fresh dill or 1 level tablespoon dried dill weed (optional)
sea salt
freshly ground pepper

Stir the grated horseradish in the cream, add the lemon juice, finely chopped dill and Tabasco. Season to taste and chill.

BALKAN SAUCE

This sauce is my own idea, but it combines ingredients often found in Hungarian cooking. It should be a lovely reddish-pink and fragrant from the seeds. Serve it with cabbage or Brussels sprouts, or as a kind of savoury with apple and Gouda cheese.

250 g/8 oz cream cheese
2 tablespoons buttermilk or yogurt
1 tablespoon mild paprika
1 tablespoon whole caraway seeds
salt
white pepper

In a bowl, soften the cream cheese, beating it with a wooden spoon. Thin with the buttermilk or yogurt. Blend in thoroughly paprika and caraway seeds. Season to taste.

WALNUT AND BASIL SAUCE

A cold sauce to serve with steamed new potatoes or cold fish.

I grow fresh basil successfully from seeds in my kitchen, in spite of the small amount of sun we get in England. But many shops now sell potted basil plants for very little, and if you look after them, snipping here and there, by the end of the summer they will have become quite bushy.

Liquid smoke is made by distilling and dissolving in water the smoke of hickory logs. (Hickory is an American hard-wood of the genus *Carya*. The wood is used in the U.S.A. for smoking hams.) Liquid smoke is highly concentrated and a very few drops produce an unusual and appetising flavour in almost any dressing or savoury dish. It is available in some bigger supermarkets or online.

60 g/2 oz walnut halves
10–12 fresh basil leaves
1 teaspoon coarse salt
3 tablespoons yogurt
3 tablespoons ricotta cheese

3 tablespoons mayonnaise
(bought will do for this)
few drops of liquid smoke
paprika and pepper to taste

In a mortar, crush together the walnuts, basil leaves and salt until well amalgamated. Stir the yogurt, ricotta and mayonnaise in a bowl. Add the basil mixture and blend well. Add the liquid smoke and season to taste.

SESAME SAUCE

A sauce to serve either cold or warm. It is particularly good with steamed Brussels sprouts. I find it more practical to toast big batches of sesame seeds in a moderately hot oven for 20 minutes, shaking the tray from time to time. They will stay crisp for months if kept in a closed jar in a dry place. In any event, they may be made crisp again if warmed in a moderate oven for 10 minutes.

2 tablespoons mayonnaise
(bought is fine for this)
2 Petit-Suisse cream cheeses

1 tablespoon toasted sesame
seeds
60 g/2 oz grated Cheddar
a pinch of cayenne pepper

Blend all the ingredients together until smooth. If the sauce is to be served warm, put the bowl in a pan of gently boiling water, where it can stay until serving time. No salt is needed.

SAUCE LAITIÈRE

Serve this sauce with hard-boiled eggs or steamed green vegetables.

125 g/4 oz cottage cheese
2–3 tablespoons natural yogurt
125 g/4 oz coarsely grated
Cheddar

a little nutmeg, freshly grated
cayenne pepper
salt
a few sorrel leaves, shredded

In a bowl which fits inside a small saucepan, mix all the ingredients except the sorrel. Boil some water in the pan, switch off the heat, put the bowl in and stir the sauce which will get creamier as the cheeses are melting. Decorate with the shredded sorrel leaves. Serve just warm.

MUSTARD SAUCE I

This sauce and the following one are to be served with pickled fish (see *gravad lax* p. 55). Both will keep well for a few days in a refrigerator.

2 egg yolks
4 tablespoons French mustard
2 tablespoons brown sugar
3 tablespoons tarragon vinegar

about 250 ml/½ pint olive oil
salt
white pepper

Cream the yolks, mustard and sugar together. Then blend in the vinegar. With a balloon whisk, gradually add the oil. Season to taste. As a side vegetable, I present a basket lined with a pretty napkin, filled with steamed baby new potatoes. They help mop up the sauce.

MUSTARD SAUCE II

This recipe is less rich than the previous one and makes a smaller quantity.

2 tablespoons caster sugar
6 tablespoons French mustard
1 tablespoon brandy
about 2 tablespoons fresh dill

2 tablespoons oil (peanut oil
would be best for this)
freshly ground black pepper

Mix all the ingredients together until well blended. Serve in a sauce-boat along with thinly sliced pickled fish and buttered pumpernickel bread.

FRESH CORIANDER SAUCE

One Friday, before going away for the week-end, I made up this recipe to avoid wasting a whole bunch of fresh coriander. It froze well, and after thinning the sauce with cream when unfrozen, I had a beautiful jade-green sauce for fresh pasta. In any event, as it contains no eggs, it will keep refrigerated for a week or so.

1 bunch fresh coriander
1 level tablespoon French
mustard

about 4 tablespoons
sunflower oil
1 tablespoon wine vinegar
salt and pepper

Cut off the roots and the bottom of the coriander stems and discard. Put the good parts, coarsely chopped, in a food processor. When the coriander is reduced to a purée, add the mustard. Run the motor again, just for a few seconds. Then scrape the sides. Run the machine again and pour the oil in through the funnel in a slow stream, as for a mayonnaise. Add the vinegar and season to taste.

Note For a good texture, when the sauce is used unfrozen, blend in 2 tablespoons of double cream or crème fraîche (p. 16).

GOOSEBERRY SAUCE

This sauce is good served hot with baked fish such as mackerel, or served cold poured over hard-boiled eggs or parboiled courgettes. It looks like a pale green mousseline sauce, smooth and fluffy. The sharpness when you taste it is a surprise.

After the sauce has been emulsified in the blender, do not reheat it or it will curdle.

500 g/1 lb gooseberries	1 egg
2 tablespoons water	salt
1 knob of butter	freshly ground white pepper
1 teaspoon demerara sugar	

In a saucepan, simmer the gooseberries with the water for 20 minutes. Off the heat, add the butter and sugar. Keep hot with a lid on. In a blender, whisk the egg until fluffy and pale. (It is important to use a blender, as you could not achieve the right texture beating by hand.) Add the hot gooseberries, season and run the motor at maximum speed for 2–3 minutes. The sauce will emulsify and become light in colour. Transfer to a sauce-boat and serve. Any left-over sauce may be kept refrigerated for later use.

WALNUT AND ANCHOVY SAUCE WITH CRUDITÉS

This is an ideal main course for a hot summer day. Serve the sauce in a pretty bowl in the middle of a large serving dish as the centre-piece on your table. Around the bowl, on the dish, place a selection of fresh and parboiled vegetables: raw carrots, celery, Chinese cabbage, cucumber, chicory, cherry tomatoes; parboiled French beans, mange-tout, cauliflower florets, and broccoli. Hard-boiled eggs in their shell may be added too. Everyone picks a bit of this, a piece of that with their fingers and dips into the sauce. The elderflower sorbet (p. 155) would make a good end to the meal.

FOR ABOUT 12 PEOPLE

250 ml/½ pint olive oil
250 g/8 oz unsalted butter
6 cloves garlic, chopped finely
and the green shoot removed
1 large handful of freshly shelled

walnuts, broken, not chopped
1 small tin anchovy fillets,
shredded
250 ml/½ pint single cream
freshly ground pepper

In a heavy enamel saucepan, put the oil and butter along with the garlic and heat gently until the garlic is golden, but not brown. Add the walnut pieces and the shredded anchovy. Stir with a wooden spoon. When the mixture is slightly thickened, add the cream. Bring just to the boil and take off the heat immediately, otherwise the cream might curdle. Season. Serve warm.

SIAMESE SAUCE

This Thai sauce is normally served with saté (little wooden skewers of pork or beef) but I find it equally delicious with a selection of crudités – try raw mange-tout peas, radishes, raw courgette sticks or cauliflower florets – or as a dip with toasted bread and biscuits.

Coconut and peanuts go well together. Peanut butter is so easy to prepare in a Magimix that I like to make my own (using the roasted unhulled sort). If you buy a block of coconut cream it keeps indefinitely in the refrigerator.

½ packet (125 g/4 oz) coconut
cream
about 250 ml/½ pint hot water
1 pot (about 350 g/12 oz)
crunchy peanut butter
1 tablespoon chilli paste

1 tablespoon demerara sugar
1 tablespoon onion juice (use a
citrus squeezer)
1 tablespoon soy sauce
sea salt
pepper

Melt the coconut cream with hot water in a heavy saucepan. Add the peanut butter, chilli paste, demerara sugar, onion juice and soy sauce.

Taste and season. Keep warm on a simmering plate or in a bain-marie, taking care not to let the sauce boil.

SAUCE BÂTARDE

To me, this sauce is as good as hollandaise, but not so rich and therefore more digestible. The addition of flour makes it less likely to curdle. The quantity of butter is absolutely flexible to suit your taste. At the very end you can add a squeeze of lemon or a dash of vinegar. This sauce is particularly good with asparagus or fish. If it is to be served with fish, instead of water use fish stock, checking the saltiness of the latter.

1 tablespoon butter	white pepper
1 tablespoon flour	60–200 g/2–7 oz butter
about 125 ml/¼ pint water	lemon juice or vinegar
2 egg yolks	(optional)
salt	

Make a roux: melt the butter, take off the heat and beat in the flour, then the hot (but not boiling) water. Still beating, add the egg yolks and a little salt and pepper. Return the pan to a gentle heat whisking constantly (I use a birch-twig whisk as it doesn't ruin the saucepan). When it begins to thicken, remove from the heat and beat in the quantity of butter desired. Keep warm in a bain-marie until needed.

CHICKEN LIVER DRESSING

This is a luscious, creamy sauce. It is not unlike the French *saupiquet*, a sauce traditionally made by the men when they come back from shooting, using the fresh raw livers of the rabbits they have shot. My version, however, uses chicken livers, lightly cooked.

You can serve this dressing with a plain roast chicken, but I like it best with a salad of raw mushrooms (sliced sideways, leaving the stalks on so they remain mushroom-shaped) and chopped watercress, seasoned with lemon juice, salt and pepper. The sharpness of the lemon and watercress balances the rich taste of the sauce. The firm raw mushrooms are a nice contrast to the smooth texture.

7 tablespoons olive oil	2 hard-boiled eggs
4 chicken livers	2 tablespoons sherry vinegar
1 garlic clove, chopped very fine	few green peppercorns, crushed
1 teaspoon *moutarde de Meaux*	in a mortar
(or other mild, whole-seed	salt to taste
mustard)	

Heat 2 tablespoons of the olive oil. Prick the livers to keep them from sputtering while cooking, and sauté lightly with the garlic until they just begin to brown. Turn out the livers and pan drippings into a food processor. Add the mustard, eggs and vinegar. Blend for a few seconds. With the motor still running, pour in the remaining oil in a stream. You should have a very smooth dressing, rather like a mayonnaise. Stir in the coarsely crushed green peppercorns. Reserve until needed, but do not chill.

FRUITS AND FLOWERS

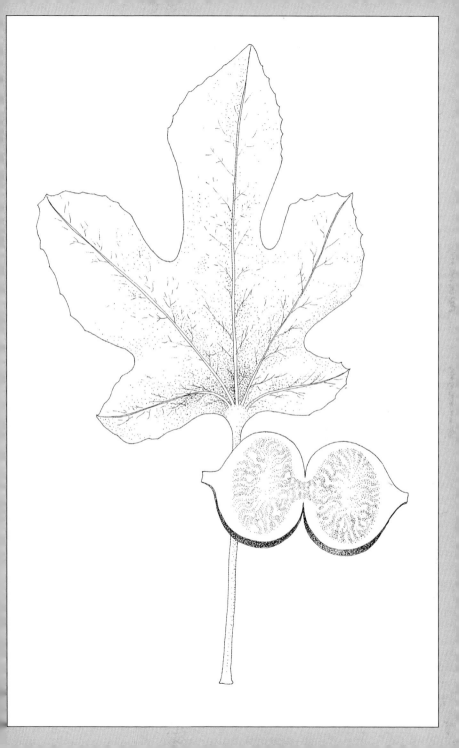

And we came to the Isle of Fruits: all round from the cliffs
   and the capes,
Purple or amber, dangled a hundred fathom of grapes,
And the warm melon lay like a little sun on the tawny sand,
And the fig ran up from the beach and rioted over the land,
And the mountain arose like a jewell'd throne thro' the fragrant air,
Glowing with all-colour'd plums and with golden masses of pear,
And crimson and scarlet of berries that flamed upon bine and vine . . .
              Alfred, Lord Tennyson, *The Voyage of Maeldune*

ORANGE SALAD

This simplest of all fruit salads is unusual with a rather intriguing taste.
If you can, prepare it several hours in advance.

6 large, juicy oranges	½ teaspoon angostura bitters

Peel the oranges, removing pith and pips. Slice the fruits on a plate, in
order to catch the juice that escapes. Arrange the slices, overlapping, on
a pretty dish. Sprinkle with the angostura, pour over the reserved juice
and chill.

FRAISES AU BEAUMES DE VENISE

Beaumes de Venise is the name of a small French town situated near
Avignon. The fruity, sweet and fragrant white wine produced there (not
unlike a Château Yquem or a Barsac, but not as expensive!) is a perfect
ending to a meal. In this recipe, it makes a glorious, but uncomplicated
dessert.

500 g/1 lb strawberries, stems removed	¾ bottle Beaumes de Venise, chilled
	about 10 mint leaves

If the strawberries are big, cut them in two. Divide them between 6 cups or little individual soup bowls. Pour over the chilled wine. With some scissors, shred the mint leaves on top. Serve chilled.

FIGS IN A VELVET COAT

A hundred mysteries concealed by the fruit from my senses, but not from my intellect.

Marcel Proust, *A la Recherche du Temps Perdu. VII*

The sensual nature of a fresh fig is evident the moment you slice it, and even more so when you sink your teeth into it. They are delicious warm from the sun, and the tiny seeds burst under the pressure of the tongue. When cut they have visual appeal: the purple outer layer, then a thin white line, and finally the glossy, crimson flesh formed by the seeds.

Sadly, it is rare in England to find perfect, scented, sweet figs. Therefore I think that in this recipe the white velvety sauce improves their taste. It works beautifully, is simple to make and the result is surprisingly subtle.

125 ml/¼ pint yogurt
125 ml/¼ pint double cream
2 tablespoons brandy
1 tablespoon crème de cacao
(cocoa liqueur)
12 figs
a few borage flowers (optional)

In a bowl, blend together the yogurt, cream, brandy and crème de cacao. Chill. Wash, pat dry and quarter the figs, removing the top of the stem. Divide equally among 6 delicate crystal cups, cover with the velvety sauce and chill for at least 2 hours, or, even better, overnight to allow the alcohol to penetrate the figs. If you have some borage, use the purple flowers scattered over to decorate; they have a sweet taste and are delicious.

WINTER PEAR SALAD

A mixture of stewed dried fruits makes a good winter salad, but dried pears are so fragrant that I use them alone for this. Red peppercorns add a subtle, spicy note.

500 g/1 lb dried pear halves	1 tablespoon orange-flower
1 stick of cinnamon	water
China tea	1 teaspoon red peppercorns
60 g/2 oz granulated sugar	(optional, see p. 114)

In a bowl cover the pears and cinnamon with hot China tea, and leave for a couple of hours or up to 12 hours. Transfer to an enamelled saucepan, add the sugar and simmer for 20 minutes. Leave to cool. Discard the cinnamon stick and stir in the orange-flower water. Serve in a glass bowl with the red peppercorns (if used) floating on top.

COCONUT, ORANGE AND DATE SALAD

This salad comes to the table as if covered by a recent fall of snow. It is worth using fresh coconut, as its flavour is better, but if you use the desiccated sort, moisten it first with a little water, blending it in with your finger tips. As far as the dates are concerned, fresh or dried may be used; the fresh ones, of course, are less sweet.

1 whole coconut, grated	4 oranges
(or 250 g/8 oz desiccated,	about 20 dates, fresh or dried
moistened with a little water)	½ glass caster sugar

To open the coconut, tap the three soft areas (darker spots) on the top with a sharp instrument. Pour out the milk and reserve. Hold the coconut in one hand and with the other tap all over with a hammer until the hard shell cracks and falls off. Separate the meat from the shell with a sharp knife. Peel the brown skin from the flesh and grate.

Peel the oranges and slice thinly, reserving pieces of zest from one. Pit and slice the dates across. In a heavy saucepan, boil half a glass of water (or coconut milk) for 2–3 minutes with the same volume of caster sugar and the reserved zest. Discard the zest and allow the syrup to cool.

In a shallow dish with straight sides, arrange a layer of oranges, then a layer of dates. Repeat the operation. Drizzle over the syrup. Sprinkle over the grated coconut, concealing completely the orange and date layers. Chill for at least 2 hours.

CURRIED MELON

This melon may be served as a light ending for a meal. It can also be a starter with a few prawns added to it. The sweet juice of the melon marries well with the curry. The contrast between the chilled fruit and spicy sauce makes this the kind of combination that I always find appealing. Do not substitute curry powder for the curry paste as the former has a rather bitter after-taste and a raspy texture.

It is fun to present the melon in a rather dramatic way, standing it in a deepish glass dish, surrounded with crushed ice. If I have some flowers, I pluck a few petals and place them here and there on the ice. Pomegranate seeds make an attractive decoration too.

1 large ripe honeydew melon   125 ml/¼ pint double cream
1 heaped teaspoon curry paste

Cut off a hat from one end of the melon and scoop out the seeds with a spoon, leaving the inside cavity free from any fibrous bits. Now scoop out the flesh, with a ball-shaped utensil preferably, put in a bowl and chill both melon shell and flesh until serving time. Blend the curry paste into the cream and chill.

Assemble the dish at the last minute: pour the spicy cream over the melon balls and refill the shell with the mixture. You may have to cut a slice off the bottom of the melon to stand it upright safely. Serve chilled.

FIG AND BACON SAVOURY

This is another variation on devils on horseback in which the thin slices of bacon are wrapped around dried figs rather than prunes. I buy Turkish figs, plump and moist, from good wholefood shops.

Allow one rasher per fig. Cut off the hard stem of each fig, then wrap the bacon around it, either securing it with a cocktail stick or just laying it carefully, seam down, in an ovenproof dish. Bake in a hot oven for 7–10 minutes.

This makes a good snack before going out, say, to the theatre, when you are planning to eat later than usual.

FRESH DATES WITH STILTON

A kind of savoury which is made in a matter of minutes. We are now quite familiar with very large fresh Californian dates, which can be found all the year around. The flavour of the dates mellows the bite of the Stilton. If you prefer a milder tasting cheese use Wensleydale instead.

125 g/4 oz Stilton cheese   500 g/1 lb fresh Californian dates

Slit each date lengthways, remove the stone and replace it by a small piece of Stilton, making bite-sized sandwiches. Place in little wicker baskets, or on a tray or platter, lined with leaves. (I use mulberry leaves.)

COOKING WITH FLOWERS

Garden that hee would vouchsafe to graunte unto you the sweete savour of his chiefe frangrante floures, that is his comfort to cleave fast unto you, his mercy to keepe you and his grace to guyde you now and evermore.

Lord Burghley, *The Gardeners Labyrinth*, 1577
Epistle dedicatory addressed to William Cecil

At first thought this might sound precious or unpractical, but it is only a question of using the imagination. Edible flowers are readily available and very easy to use.

PURPLE OMELETTE

In spring, gather a few of the purplish-blue flowers of the chive plant. They taste delicately of onion. The contrast between the colour of the flowers and the colour of the eggs makes for a very bold effect.

5 eggs

2 tablespoons soda water

½ teaspoon sea salt

dash of cayenne pepper

2 tablespoons chopped parsley

1 handful of chive flowers

Separate the spiky petals of the flowers and reserve. Prepare the omelette in the usual way, using all the other ingredients. (The soda water makes the omelette lighter.) At the last minute, scatter the petals over the pan. Fold the omelette, and transfer to a warmed serving dish.

NASTURTIUM AND AVOCADO SALAD

This is a salad of contrasts: first the green and vermilion colouring, secondly the bland and piquant taste, and lastly the smooth and crunchy textures. Nasturtium leaves have a tartness similar to those of the Good King Henry plant, a few of which can be added to the salad.

2–3 ripe but firm avocado pears

5 nasturtium flowers

a few nasturtium leaves

(optional)

3 tablespoons emulsified

vinaigrette (p. 134)

sprinkling of cayenne pepper

Prepare this salad at the last minute, as the peeled avocados will discolour quickly. In any case, cover and refrigerate until serving.

Cut the avocado pears in half, lengthways, then peel and stone them. Cut in long slices. On a round serving dish of contrasting colour, spread the slices in a circle, like the petals of a flower. Spoon over the dressing. Arrange the nasturtium flowers on the top. If you are using them, chop the leaves in thin strands and sprinkle over. Dust with cayenne pepper.

MARROW-FLOWER BEIGNETS

In Aix-en-Provence, the stalls at the farmers' market sell bunches of these flowers, and this recipe is quite common there.

If you have a kitchen garden, pick the flowers after the fruit is formed before they drop off of their own accord. Using the flowers this way will not harm the plant. I once tried to draw them in my cookbook from memory, but found I could not remember all the details of their complicated structure: the hairy, horn-shaped stems, the green-shaded ribs blending into the twisted orange petals which end in a point. Marrow flowers can be replaced by courgette flowers, which are more widely grown now. Whichever you use, the dish should be made rapidly after picking the flowers or they wilt. I find that soda water or beer makes a lighter batter.

150 g/5 oz plain flour	8–10 marrow flowers
1 egg	granulated sugar
pinch of salt	pepper
2 tablespoons olive oil	oil for deep frying
soda water or beer	1 lemon cut in long wedges

Mix together the flour, egg, salt, oil and enough soda water or beer to make a light batter. Whisk well and leave to rest for 2 hours.

Cut the marrow flowers in half lengthways and remove the stalk and calyx. Dip the flowers in the batter and fry in deep oil until golden brown. Drain on absorbent paper. Sprinkle with sugar, dust with pepper. Serve as soon as possible with the lemon slices.

MARIGOLD AND CAULIFLOWER

Shakespeare's 'winking mary-buds' are marigolds (*Calendula officinalis*) which are found in many gardens. The taste has a slight aromatic bitterness.

Marigold petals were used as a herb long ago and the marigold's dense colour gave many dishes their golden hue. In fresh and dried form it appeared in puddings, cakes and salads. Nowadays it is used mainly as a natural colorant for butter and cheese. For the winter, you can get dried flowers from a herbalist. Their orange petals will enliven a green salad or brighten an egg dish.

1 medium-sized cauliflower	2 sprigs fresh parsley, coarsely
1 tablespoon dried marigold	chopped
petals, crushed	a few fresh marigold petals
60 g/2 oz butter	salt and pepper

Cut a cross in the bottom of the cauliflower stalks to ensure that it cooks evenly. Lower it into a saucepan filled with salted, boiling water. Add the crushed dried marigold petals and cook for 10–12 minutes. The cauliflower should be tender and still crisp, and lightly coloured by the petals. Drain and put into a hot dish. Smear with fresh butter and season. Scatter here and there the chopped parsley and the fresh petals.

GERANIUM CREAM

This is a velvety and luscious cream, flavoured with the scented leaves of the rose geranium. It should be served chilled to accompany any soft summer fruits, or on its own with brittle almond biscuits.

250 ml/½ pint double cream or	4–5 sweet-scented rose
crème fraîche (p. 16)	geranium leaves
4 tablespoons caster sugar	250 g/8 oz cream cheese or
	fromage blanc (p. 16)

Put the cream in a double saucepan with the sugar and the geranium leaves, and cook gently until the cream is hot but not boiling. Leave to cool and then mix thoroughly with the cream cheese or fromage blanc until smooth. Cover and chill overnight. Take out the geranium leaves just before serving.

ELDERFLOWER SORBET

This sorbet is nearly as good made with dried flowers as with fresh ones. In London, they can be obtained from Baldwin's, the herbalist (www. baldwins.co.uk), all the year round. However there is nothing more fun than picking the fresh flowers in season from hedgerows in little country roads, particularly if there is a ditch between you and the inaccessible bush! Elder is too often treated as a nuisance, but its scented lychee flavour is too good to be overlooked. The sorbet is a refreshing end to a rich meal and the elusive taste will puzzle your guests.

6–8 fresh elderflower heads or 2 heaped tablespoons dried ones	750 ml/1½ pints water 150 g/4½ oz sugar juice and rind of 4 lemons

If using fresh flowers, wash and pat them dry to remove any insects. In a heavy metal saucepan, heat the water and sugar gently until the syrup is clear. Take off the fire and infuse flowers, lemon juice and rind in the syrup for 1 hour. Strain. Pour into a metal tray and freeze. When the mixture begins to set, blend or whip well and return to the freezer. Repeat 2 or 3 times at intervals to break up the ice crystals. If using an ice-cream maker, follow the manufacturer's instructions, If the sorbet is very hard, let it soften for 40–50 minutes in the refrigerator before serving.

PUDDINGS

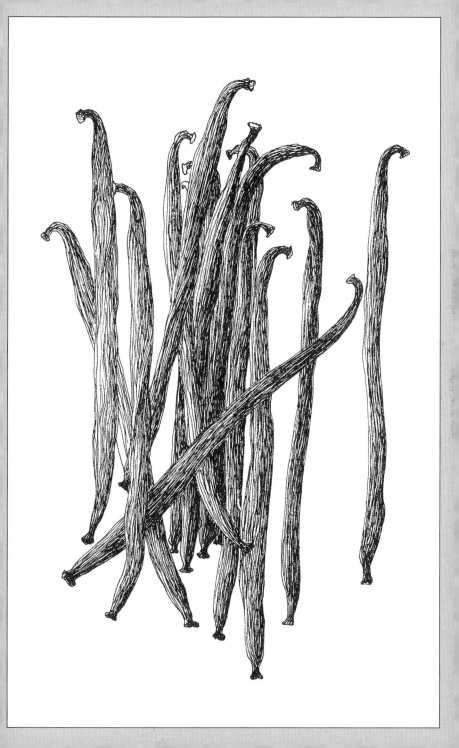

SMOKED TEA ICE CREAM
WITH CRYSTALLISED MINT LEAVES

A very rich ice cream which has an unusual smoky flavour given by Lapsang Souchong tea. I buy the best quality, usually sold loose. It may seem quite expensive, but use it sparingly and you will see that only a small amount is necessary to give the most gorgeous aroma.

For most puddings I use caster sugar kept in a large jar with several vanilla pods tucked in to flavour it.

The unused egg whites can be used to make crystallised mint leaves for decoration (instructions at the end of the recipe) or *petits coeurs aux amandes* (p. 172) to serve with coffee.

500 ml/1 pint rich milk	175 g/6 oz vanilla-flavoured
3 level tablespoons Lapsang	caster sugar
Souchong tea	2 egg whites
1 tablespoon rose-water	1 tablespoon water
6 large egg yolks	

In a saucepan, heat the milk slowly (do not boil), add the tea leaves and leave simmering for 15 minutes. Stir in the rose-water. In another pan, put the egg yolks and 125 g/4 oz of the sugar, and beat with a wooden spoon until the mixture becomes white and frothy; then little by little add the strained milk. Put the pan on a simmering mat and whisk until the mixture has the consistency of custard and coats the spoon. Do not let it boil or it will curdle. Cool and chill.

Meanwhile, beat the egg whites until they are stiff. Add the remaining sugar to the water in a heavy saucepan and stir until dissolved. Boil over a gentle heat for 2 minutes and immediately pour in a fine stream onto the egg whites, beating constantly until the mixture is cool. (The egg whites will have set and become glossy.) Chill. Blend with the custard mixture and freeze for at least 3 hours.

About 45 minutes before serving, put the ice cream in the refrigerator. Serve decorated with crystallised mint leaves (see next recipe).

CRYSTALLISED MINT LEAVES

I egg white, beaten   caster sugar
whole mint leaves

Paint all the leaves with the beaten egg white, making sure they are completely coated, then sprinkle thoroughly with caster sugar. Put on a cake-rack in a warm place to dry for a few hours before storing in airtight jars. They will keep for 2–3 days.

CASSATA DI RICOTTA

Here is another way to use the versatile ricotta cheese. In this semi-frozen pudding it has a taste and texture all its own. As far as the liqueur is concerned, I have tried Crème de Cacao and Tia Maria, and both were very interesting indeed, but if you prefer not to be adventurous, use Cointreau or Grand Marnier.

The cassata may be prepared in advance and chilled, but to get the right half-frozen texture, it should be put in the freezer part of the refrigerator about 2 hours before serving. I freeze the cassata in a china dish in which it will be brought to the table, decorated with transparent green sticks of candied angelica which contrast with the white cheese, dotted with the black chocolate bits.

500 g/1 lb ricotta
4 tablespoons caster sugar
3 tablespoons sour cream or
    crème fraîche (p. 16)
3 tablespoons liqueur

3 tablespoons chopped angelica,
    plus a piece for decoration
60 g/2 oz bitter chocolate,
    chopped coarsely (a packet
    of chocolate chips will do)

Beat well the ricotta, sugar and sour cream or crème fraîche, add the liqueur and keep on beating until the mixture is smoothly blended. Fold in the chopped angelica, reserving a piece for the decoration, and the chocolate bits. Pile onto a china serving dish. Put in the freezer for about 2 hours or until half-frozen. Decorate with little sticks of the angelica stuck in here and there.

CHOCOLATE DECADENCE

An iced pudding which is unanimously liked, even by people who haven't a sweet tooth. Cardamom seeds add an exotic touch to the bitter taste of cocoa. It seems elaborate, but in fact it is child's play to make. Always serve with a tumbler of iced water to drink.

4 cardamom pods
250 ml/½ pint double cream
100 g/3 oz vanilla sugar
3 large eggs
2 tablespoons hot water

5 tablespoons cocoa powder
(Dutch preferably)
1 tablespoon instant coffee
powder
4 tablespoons sour cream
1 tablespoon whisky

Remove the pods and crush the cardamom seeds in a mortar. In a bowl, beat together the double cream, sugar, eggs and cardamom seeds until smooth. Stir together the hot water, the cocoa powder and instant coffee, making a smooth paste, and add it to the cream and egg mixture. Put the bowl over a pan of simmering water, stirring constantly until the custard coats the back of a spoon. Remove from the heat and allow to cool, stirring from time to time. Then add the sour cream and whisky. Pour into a container (preferably made of metal, which is a better heat conductor), cover and freeze. As this pudding doesn't get very hard it may be served straight from the freezer.

You may use condensed milk instead of cream, but then omit the sugar and add a few drops of pure vanilla essence.

FRESH MINT ICE CREAM

I had this ice cream for the first time when staying with friends in Scotland. Part of their kitchen garden was overgrown with mint plants of various kinds and this recipe was a good way to use them up. The ice cream was made with a blend of apple mint and lemon mint. This mixture imparted a subtle freshness to the ice cream. I have tried it since with the usual spearmint found in greengrocers' and thought the result quite delicious too.

When I feel extravagant, I present the moulded green ice cream on a tray made of ice as follows: fill a flan tin with dyed water (I use a food dye, normally red or violet) and freeze. Before serving, turn out the coloured block and place the ice cream in the centre.

ENOUGH FOR 8–10 PEOPLE

250 g/8 oz caster sugar
250 ml/½ pint water
2 handfuls mint leaves, stripped
off the stems

juice of 2 lemons
about 250 ml/½ pint double
cream

Bring the water and sugar slowly to the boil, stirring until dissolved. Boil for 3 minutes and leave to cool. Put the mint leaves in a blender and pour in the syrup while blending. Strain through a nylon sieve, extracting as much minty syrup as possible (the last drops are in fact the strongest in colour and flavour). Add the strained lemon juice. Pour into a shallow tray and freeze until mushy, about 1 hour, then put back in the blender and process until light and a little frothy. Fold in the lightly whipped cream (a little less cream may be used if you don't want it too rich). Freeze for a few hours. It is best to put the ice cream in the refrigerator for an hour before serving to let it soften properly. If you forget, leave it at room temperature for 15 minutes.

CINNAMON CREAM

This frozen cream can be served as an accompaniment to gooseberry cake (p. 170) or pears stewed in red wine. It can also be made into a pudding in its own right by adding a stiffly beaten egg white and a little more sugar to the mixture before freezing. The spice gives a lovely tinge to the cream, with tiny cinnamon-coloured speckles.

250 ml/½ pint double cream
1 tablespoon cold water
about 5 tablespoons caster sugar

1 teaspoon powdered cinnamon or ½ teaspoon natural cinnamon flavour (from good grocers)

Chill the cream and water in a mixing bowl for 1 hour in a refrigerator or 10 minutes in a freezer. Chill the whisk too. Then whisk until thick and nearly tripled in volume. Fold in the cinnamon and sugar, pour into a small soufflé dish and freeze for at least 5 hours. Serve straight from the freezer as the mixture has a semi-soft, creamy consistency.

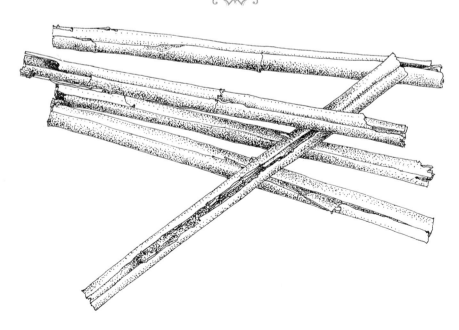

STEAMED FIG PUDDING

I remember the open market at Argentan, in Normandy, one glorious Sunday morning. The market was held in the church square, the bells were tolling and everybody was chatty and gay. My eye was caught by one stall in particular and I rushed over to it. An old lady was selling bagfuls of dried fruits, nuts, homemade biscuits and dates on the stalk. But what I had noticed was some shiny, partly dried figs, strung together with raffia. I bought several strings – *chapelets* as she called them. They were probably the best I have ever had.

The only problem with this pudding is that I never make enough of it. Though people worry about the high calorie content of steamed puddings, it doesn't seem to stop them eating this one. I carefully balance the meal with light courses like jellied watercress and apple soup (p. 80) followed by *poulet à la croûte au sel* (p. 73). I buy dried figs from Turkey.

These quantities make enough to fill two 500-n l/1-pint pudding basins or one 1-litre/2-pint basin.

500 g/1 lb dried figs	350 g/12 oz shredded suet
500 ml/1 pint milk	250 g/8 oz granulated sugar
250 g/8 oz self-raising flour	3 large eggs
1 teaspoon each mace and cinnamon	100 g/3 oz fresh breadcrumbs grated rind of 2 oranges
½ teaspoon salt	

Stem and coarsely chop the figs. Rinse a heavy saucepan in cold water and put in the milk and figs. Bring just to boiling point over a very low heat and simmer, stirring, for 20 minutes. Leave to cool.

In a bowl, sift together the flour, spices and salt. In a different large bowl, cream together the shredded suet and sugar until fluffy. Add the eggs, one at a time, beating well after each addition, and stir in the fresh breadcrumbs and orange rind. Add the flour mixture alternately with the fig mixture, beating well. Pour into a well buttered pudding basin (or two if using small ones). Cover tightly with foil and secure with string.

Put the basin in a large pan and fill it half way up the sides of the basin with hot water. (I put the basin on a standing ring, sold specially for this purpose, which allows the water to move freely under the basin.) Cover the pan and steam the pudding over moderate heat for 2 hours (a little less for small ones, say about 1¼ hours). Remove from the pan and leave to cool, covered, for 20 minutes. Remove the string and foil and invert the pudding onto a shallow dish. Serve with cinnamon cream (p. 162).

TARTE AUX POMMES D'AGNÈS

I use a very large, round, shallow dish or tin for this cake. It looks more impressive that way. The delicacy of the cake depends on the batter for the base being spread thinly. The coating added at the second stage becomes golden and shiny and sometime crackles, making a rather interesting effect.

BASE

5 level tablespoons flour	½ teaspoon baking powder
4 heaped tablespoons caster sugar	1 large egg
3 tablespoons milk	a pinch of salt
2 tablespoons thin oil (sunflower)	2 eating apples (Russets are best for this)

GLAZE

80 g/2½ oz butter, melted and slightly cooled	flavoured with vanilla
100 g/3 oz caster sugar,	1 large egg

Pre-heat the oven to gas 4/350°F/180°C. In a small bowl, beat thoroughly the ingredients for the base (except the apples), making sure that no lumps remain. Grease a round, shallow, ovenproof dish or tin, about 40 cm/16 inches in diameter, and smear with the mixture. Arrange the peeled and thinly sliced apples all over in an attractive pattern and bake for 25 minutes.

Meanwhile, prepare the glaze by mixing the sugar and egg into the cooled melted butter.

After the first 25 minutes in the oven, take the tart out and pour the glaze evenly over the apple. Bake for a further 15 minutes. Serve warm or cold.

ORANGE-FLOWER AND CREAM CHEESE FROSTING

This icing is not too sweet and could be used to cover the gooseberry cake (p. 170) or served frozen with steamed fig pudding (p. 163). The orange-flower water gives it an exotic and old-fashioned taste.

250 g/8 oz cream cheese
60 g/2 oz margarine or butter
500 g/1 lb vanilla sugar

1 tablespoon orange-flower water

Leave the cream cheese and margarine or butter to soften at room temperature. Then, in a bowl, cream them with the other ingredients until smooth. Use as required.

TEA TIME

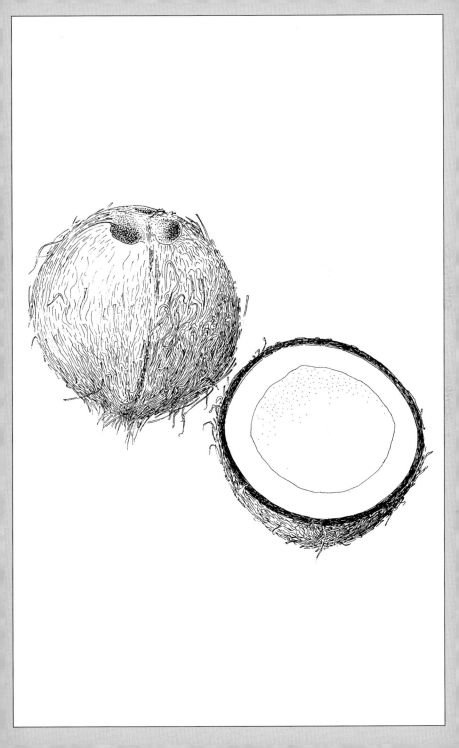

COCONUT AND ORANGE CAKE

This cake, although not rich, is moist and dense, with the exotic flavours of coconut and anise combined. For a real treat, use freshly grated coconut (if doing so, omit the water and first stage of the recipe). This cake keeps well for a week or so if covered and put in a refrigerator.

For a birthday cake, double the quantity and bake two cakes. Use as a filling and as icing the orange-flower and cream cheese frosting on page 165.

175 g/6 oz desiccated coconut (or freshly grated)	pinch of salt
1 tablespoon water	100 g/3 oz butter
finely grated rind of 1 large orange	125 g/4 oz caster sugar
175 g/6 oz flour	1 teaspoon vanilla essence
½ tablespoon baking powder	1 large egg
	125 ml/¼ pint milk
	1 tablespoon aniseeds

Sprinkle the desiccated coconut with the water and using a fork, make sure it is all thoroughly moistened. Add the orange rind and set aside.

Pre-heat the oven to gas 5/375°F/190°C. Butter a 20-cm/8-inch round cake tin. Dust it all over lightly with flour, shaking out any excess. Reserve.

Sift together flour, baking powder and salt. Cream the butter and sugar, add the vanilla essence and the egg and beat until smooth. Add the dry ingredients in stages, alternately with the milk. Scrape the bowl with a spatula as necessary and beat until smooth after each addition. Stir in the coconut and orange mixture. Put in the prepared cake tin, tilting and shaking the tin gently to level the batter. Bake for 20–25 minutes. Leave to cool. Invert onto a rack and then again onto a serving dish.

TARTE JAPONAISE

I do not know quite why this tart is called *japonaise*. I learnt it from a friend in Paris whose cook came from Vietnam and this was her name for it. She uses walnuts, but I prefer to substitute hazelnuts as they have a more delicate flavour, particularly when they are lightly toasted as in this recipe. The filling comes out deliciously crisp. The pie will keep quite well, but I never seem to have any left after a dinner party. This tart should be served with a jug of sour cream.

FOR THE PASTRY FLAN

150 g/5 oz flour
1 heaped tablespoon caster sugar

100 g/3 oz butter, at room temperature
about 2 tablespoons iced water

FOR THE FILLING

100 g/3 oz whole hazelnuts
100 g/3 oz butter
60 g/2 oz desiccated coconut
100 g/3 oz currants

1 teaspoon wine vinegar
½ teaspoon pure vanilla extract
sour cream

Pre-heat the oven to gas 4/350°F/180°C. At the same time put a baking sheet on the centre shelf to get hot. Toast the hazelnuts for 15 minutes in the oven. While still hot, rub off their skins (I do this with oven gloves on, winnowing the flakes over the sink by blowing gently). Chop the nuts coarsely. Reserve.

Now make your pastry. Sift the flour and sugar into a large bowl. Cut the butter into the flour and rub in lightly with the fingertips until it looks like breadcrumbs. With a round-bladed knife mix in a little iced water until the mixture only just begins to hold together. Gather into a ball and leave to rest for about 10 minutes.

In a saucepan, melt the butter and add all the other ingredients except the sour cream, tossing to ensure that the nuts and fruit are evenly coated. Reserve.

Roll out the pastry and line a 25-cm/10-inch flan dish. Spread over the filling, put the tart on to the baking sheet (this helps the pastry to cook more crisply underneath) and bake for 25–30 minutes. Serve lukewarm or cold with the sour cream separately.

GOOSEBERRY CAKE

In this cake, the gooseberry flavour is delicate, but noticeable. The gooseberry purée can be flavoured with elderflower to give an extra fragrance to the cake. Dark muscovado sugar (the least refined cane sugar available) and wholemeal flour are a good combination and they make this cake very moist and nutty. The recipe works well with apples instead of gooseberries.

175 g/6 oz dark muscovado sugar	raising flour (or wholemeal flour
125 g/4 oz butter or margarine	sifted with 1½ teaspoons baking powder)
1 large egg	1 teaspoon each nutmeg and allspice
250 ml/½ pint unsweetened gooseberry purée	a pinch of ground cloves
150 g/5 oz wholemeal self-	

Pre-heat the oven to gas 5/375°F/190°C. Grease a cake tin 25 cm/10 inches in diameter and line the bottom with nonstick paper. (Bakewell brand is best for this.)

Cream sugar and butter or margarine until pale yellow and fluffy. Add the lightly beaten egg. Stir in the gooseberry purée. Sieve all the dry ingredients together and add them gradually to the gooseberry mixture. Put in the tin and bake for 45 minutes. Cool before inverting onto a cake plate. Serve with cinnamon cream (p. 162) and stewed gooseberries.

GROUND RICE CAKE

After a bad illness, I went to spend some time with friends in Nairobi. After a week of not cooking, I could no longer resist going into the kitchen and experimenting with new dishes, inspired by the abundance of fruits and vegetables. I was always ready to go to the market to see the overflowing baskets of limes, passion fruits and pineapples. The first thing I made was this old stand-by of mine, which I had made so many times in London. Njenga, the cook, was thrilled to be shown new dishes. This cake reminds me of the beginning of our friendship and four-handed collaboration. We had three or four failures to start with, because of the altitude and climate there. The cake didn't react as usual, but when mastered again it was made every day for tea, and the remaining few slices would disappear at the breakfast table the following day.

125 g/4 oz butter or margarine
250 g/8 oz caster sugar
125 g/4 oz ground rice
grated rind of 1 orange and 1 lemon
125 g/4 oz self-raising flour
2 eggs

Pre-heat the oven to gas 4/350°F/180°C. Line a loaf tin, approximately 25 x 10 x 10 cm/10 x 4 x 4 inches, with greaseproof paper or foil. Grease and flour the sides and bottom, shaking out any excess flour. Cream together the butter or margarine and caster sugar. Add the ground rice and rind, and then add alternately the self-raising flour and lightly beaten eggs. Pour into the prepared tin and bake on the middle shelf of the oven for 1 hour.

PETITS COEURS AUX AMANDES

I felt suddenly... a bitter-sweet fragrance of almond steal towards me from the hawthorn blossom, and then I noticed that on the flowers themselves were little spots of a creamier colour, in which I imagined that this fragrance must lie concealed, as the taste of an almond cake lay in the burned parts.

Marcel Proust, *A la Recherche du Temps Perdu. I*

The delicacy of these small heart-shaped cakes depends on heating the butter properly. It should reach the nutty-smelling stage called *noisette* in French. I serve them at tea time with a light-scented China tea; their effect on me is equivalent to that of the little *madeleines* on Proust.

60 g/2 oz flour	4 egg whites
60 g/2 oz ground almonds	100 g/3 oz unsalted butter
150 g/5 oz vanilla sugar	

Pre-heat the oven to gas 6–7/400–425°F/200–220°C. Butter generously 12 heart-shaped cake tins, about 8 cm/3½ inches in diameter.

Sift together in a bowl the flour, ground almonds and vanilla sugar. Make a well in the centre and pour in the egg whites. With a wooden spoon, gradually incorporate the dry ingredients into the whites. In a small, heavy saucepan, heat the butter until it is a light golden colour and smells nutty. Let it cool for a minute and then add to the other ingredients. Half-fill the cake tins with the warm mixture. Bake for 18–20 minutes, checking the colour and covering with baking foil if the tops get too brown. Leave to cool in the moulds before removing.

※

COCOA AND COGNAC CANDIES

These fudge-like little squares freeze well. Serve them for tea or with coffee at the end of a meal. The cognac takes a little of the sweetness away and the ginger biscuits contribute a spicy note. These candies are speedily made as no cooking is involved.

250 g/8 oz ginger nut biscuits
125 g/4 oz butter
1 tablespoon golden syrup
3 heaped tablespoons cocoa

powder
about 6 coriander seeds,
crushed finely
1 tablespoon cognac

Have ready a shallow cake tin about 12 x 20 cm/5 x 8 inches.

Put the biscuits into a plastic bag and crush them with a rolling pin (uneven-sized crumbs are rather nice, giving more crunch to the candies). Cream the butter and work in the golden syrup, cocoa powder and coriander. Mix well and blend in the biscuit crumbs. Add the cognac to the mixture. Press into the tin (it doesn't need to be greased) and chill for several hours until firm. Cut into squares and serve.

DATE AND OAT SLICES

These are easily made, and loved by children. The crunchy oat and nut outside and the soft date and orange centre make these wholesome slices very palatable indeed.

You may substitute a thick, sweetened purée of apple or rhubarb for the dates.

500 g/1 lb dates, pitted
about 2 glassfuls orange juice
½ teaspoon cinnamon
3 cardamom pods

6 cupfuls of granola (p.45)
6 tablespoons yogurt or
buttermilk

Cut the dates in two and put them into a heavy saucepan with the orange juice, cinnamon and crushed cardamom seeds. Simmer, covered, for an hour or so, adding a little more orange juice if necessary. Stir from time to time, making sure that the mixture doesn't catch at the bottom. The dates should be reduced to a thick mush.

Moisten the granola with the yogurt or buttermilk. In a square or oblong tin (30 x 20 x 4 cm/11 x 7 x 1½ inches), press down three-quarters of the granola mixture. Spoon over the date purée and spread it evenly. Cover with the remaining granola mixture, pressing gently with the back of a large spoon. Leave to stand for an hour and serve cut in long slices. These may be frozen successfully; they will require about 10 minutes to thaw at room temperature.

ALLSPICE BISCUITS

These are coal-black, crunchy and deliciously buttery and peppery. The dough may be prepared ahead of time, frozen and then sliced whenever you want to bake the biscuits. The black pepper and allspice should preferably be freshly ground. I keep the latter in a pepper mill, as its hard berries are more easily ground that way.

250 g/8 oz sifted unbleached flour	½ teaspoon cinnamon
1½ teaspoons baking powder	100 g/3 oz unsweetened cocoa powder
1 teaspoon allspice	200 g/6 oz butter
½ teaspoon finely ground black pepper	1½ teaspoons vanilla extract
a pinch of cayenne pepper	250 g/8 oz granulated sugar
	1 large egg

Sift the first 7 ingredients together and set aside. In a large bowl, cream the butter. Add the vanilla extract and sugar and beat well. Beat in the egg and gradually add the sifted dry ingredients, scraping the bowl with a rubber spatula and beating only until thoroughly mixed.

Have ready a strip of wax paper about 40 cm/16 inches long. Spoon the dough in heaped tablespoonfuls down the length of the paper, forming a sausage-like strip about 30 cm/12 inches long. Roll the dough in the paper to wrap it, pressing with your hands to shape the dough evenly. Slide a baking tray under the wrapped dough (as it might break because of its length), and transfer to the freezer or refrigerator for several hours (or longer) until firm.

Pre-heat the oven to gas 5/375°F/190°C. Line 2 baking trays

with foil. Unwrap the firm dough and with a sharp knife cut it into ½-cm/¼-inch slices. Place the slices, a little apart, on the trays. Bake for 5–6 minutes and then change the trays over on the shelves and turn them round to ensure even baking. Bake for a further 5–6 minutes. The biscuits are done when the top springs back if pressed with a fingertip. Do not overbake. With a spatula, transfer the biscuits to a rack to cool.

DAMPERS

This is a recipe I learned from an old lady who was once a Girl Guide Commissioner in Yorkshire. Dampers were a favourite on Guide picnics. They are made by taking a stick of elder or ash from a hedge, and after peeling back the bark a little, twisting a piece of dough around the green wood. This is then held over the embers of a bonfire to bake. Once the dough is a good colour, the stick is pulled from the centre to be replaced by butter and raspberry jam. Dampers are wonderfully messy to eat, as the butter melts and drips all over the fingers. At the end of the summer they can be eaten with freshly gathered blackberries which stain the hands bluish-red. I have not been able to discover the origin of the name.

125 g/4 oz self-raising flour	30 g/1 oz fat
pinch of salt	a little water

Add the salt to the flour and mix the fat into it lightly with your fingertips. Bind to a soft dough with water. Leave to rest for at least 1 hour.

Take a walnut-sized piece of dough, pull it into a long thin strip and wrap around the stick. Bake over the fire and eat hot with butter and jam.

THE
STILL-ROOM

The rule is, jam to-morrow and jam yesterday – but never jam to-day.
Lewis Carroll, *Through the Looking Glass*

There is nothing like jam to bring back the memory of childhood. How vividly I remember the array of coloured pots brought to the tea table, and the delight in our eyes when the jam was spread lavishly on a crusty, thickly buttered *tartine*.

Most of us were brought up to think that jam is only to be eaten on bread or toast, but I like eating good homemade jam on its own, from the pot, savouring the flavour of the fruit. I also find that a nearly empty jar doesn't look appetizing, so that gives me a good excuse to finish it up!

Nowadays I get as much pleasure from preparing jams as from eating them. The tantalising smell of strawberry jam cooking, or the delicate scent of quinces, these are as magical to me as is the sensuous texture of tomato jam.

Unless you are making large quantities of jam to feed hungry children, it is nicer to make small batches of jam and vary their flavours as the mood takes you. Try adding spices, herbs, seeds or nuts to them.

MARROW AND GINGER PRESERVE

When marrows are plentiful in early autumn, this is a good way to use them. The result is like crystallised ginger, except that the marrows don't have the same fibrous texture, but a soft gooey inside and crunchy exterior. Sometimes I use this preserve as a topping for vanilla ice cream.

FOR 6–7 POTS

1½–2 kg/3–3½ lb marrow	1 fresh ginger root, peeled and
1½ kg/3 lb preserving sugar	sliced

Peel and cut the marrow into 2-cm/¾-inch cubes, discarding all the seeds and woolly bits. In a large crock, alternate layers of marrow and sugar. Leave for 24 hours (this will help the marrow pieces to stay whole, instead of disintegrating into a mush during cooking), tossing from time to time.

In a preserving pan, bring to the boil the fruit and syrup, add the sliced ginger tied in a muslin bag. Simmer for 30 minutes or until the marrow pieces are translucent and amber in colour. Leave to cool and then discard the ginger bag. Ladle into clean jars, warmed gently in the oven. Cover and label.

Keep at least 3 weeks before eating in order to let the flavour mature.

GOOSEBERRY AND ELDERFLOWER JAM

The delicate, transparent green and subtle flavour of this jam make it a perfect partner for croissants.

FOR 6–7 POTS

1½ kg/3 lb green gooseberries   5–6 heads of elderflower in a
1¼ kg/2½ lb granulated sugar   muslin bag
500 ml/1 pint water

Top and tail the gooseberries. In a pan, dissolve the sugar in the water, add the elderflowers and bring to the boil. Simmer for 15–20 minutes, skimming the rising foam from time to time. Now put in the fruit and boil gently for 25–30 minutes or until the jam sets when tested on a plate. Discard the muslin bag. Ladle into clean, warmed jars. Cover with waxed paper and lid.

RHUBARB AND GINGER JAM

Even if you don't like the sharpness of stewed rhubarb, this rich spicy recipe might tempt you.

FOR 7–8 POTS

2 kg/4 lb rhubarb   100 g/3 oz crystallised ginger,
1¾ kg/3½ lb light brown sugar   chopped fine
juice of 2 lemons

Wash and dry the rhubarb stalks; cut them into 2-cm/1-inch lengths. Put in a crock in alternate layers with the sugar and leave overnight in a cool place. In the morning, the rhubarb will be covered by its own juice. Transfer the fruit and syrupy juice to a preserving pan. Add the lemon juice, bring to the boil, then reduce the heat a little to prevent it catching at the bottom. Stir frequently. After 10 minutes add the ginger pieces. Skim the rising foam from time to time. Test the jam on a plate; it should set after 30 minutes. Ladle the jam through a jam funnel into the clean, warmed pots. Leave to cool and cover.

TOMATO AND CARDAMOM JAM

The nicest way to eat this is with cream cheese or fromage blanc (p. 16). I also serve it sometimes with steamed grey mullet (p. 58). This jam is a beautiful, translucent red, like stained glass.

FOR 6–7 POTS

2 kg/4 lb red tomatoes	1 teaspoon cardamom seeds,
2 kg/4 lb sugar	ground very fine
juice and rind of 3 lemons	

Scald and drain the tomatoes. Let them cool, then peel, quarter and remove the seeds. In a large crock, put the tomatoes in layers, alternating with sugar. Leave overnight, or at least 3 hours. In a preserving pan, bring the tomatoes and the syrupy juice they have rendered to the boil with the lemon rinds and juice and spice. Skim the foam from the surface from time to time.

Have ready the clean pots which have been gently heated in the oven or on the top of the stove. (This is to prevent them cracking when the jam is poured in.) Test the jam on a plate several times until it sets. Let it cool for a few minutes, then with a jam funnel and a ladle, fill the pots. Cover and label.

Coriander seeds are a good alternative if you don't like cardamom.

QUINCE CHEESE

The quince has been cultivated for more than 4,000 years. It is a native of Persia and Anatolia and perhaps as far north as the Caucasus and as far west as Greece. The Greeks still use them in fatty dishes, in order to counteract the greasiness. Almost all other fruits have gained in favour since antiquity; the quince has moved in the opposite direction. Its taste hasn't changed, it is our gastronomic education which has done so.

Since 1870, most pears have been grown on quince rootstock. Quinces are somewhat similar in appearance, more densely yellow when fully ripe, but too hard and tart for raw consumption. This perhaps explains why they are neglected. Soft quinces are grown in Latin America, but not in Europe. Not so long ago, quinces were to be found only in private gardens, but happily they are becoming popular again and more and more greengrocers are selling them. For me, they are a most interesting and fragrant fruit.

Quince cheese makes lovely Christmas presents if, when ready, you spread it on oiled square trays and let it dry for several weeks in an airing cupboard. Cut it into 2-cm/1-inch pieces, roll them in demerara sugar, and box them in layers, separated by waxed paper. Though the method is similar, the recipe below is for potted quince cheese.

FOR ABOUT 6 POTS

1½ kg/3 lb quinces	juice and rind of 1 orange
½ glass of water	1¼ kg/2½ lb sugar

With a clean cloth, rub the fluff off the quince skins. Quarter them and put in a pan with the water, orange juice and rind. Simmer for 2–3 hours or until soft. By that time the fruits will have turned to an orangey-pink colour. Remove the cores and pass through the medium blade of a vegetable mouli. Add the sugar and leave it in the pulp for ½ hour to dissolve.

Bring the fruit to the boil in a preserving pan and keep on stirring with a long wooden spoon. Be careful that the volcano-like splatterings don't burn your hands. After 20 minutes the quince cheese should have turned a deep amber colour. Ladle into clean, warmed pots and cover immediately.

Serve with cheese or as a pudding with cream cheese. You can add 2 tablespoons of the quince cheese to warm apple purée. The flavour will scent the apples delicately.

GERANIUM JELLY

The addition of a few leaves of the scented rose geranium to apple jelly brings reminiscences of the Middle East.

FOR ABOUT 6–8 POTS

3 kg/6 lb apples
about 2–2½ kg/4–5 lb granulated sugar

10–12 leaves of the scented rose geranium

Chop the apples roughly (with their skins and pips) and put them in an earthenware pot. Fill with 2 cm/1 inch of water. Leave in a low oven for 12 hours, or until reduced to a pulp. Strain the pulp through a jelly-bag. Allow 500 g/1 lb of sugar to each 500 ml/pint of juice. Just warm the sugar in a cool oven. Meanwhile, in a preserving pan, boil the juice for 20 minutes with the rose geranium leaves. Add the warmed sugar, let it dissolve, stirring all the time. Bring to the boil and test after 1–2 minutes. Remove the leaves. Using a jam funnel, pour into clean, warmed jars. Cover immediately and label.

PÂTE DE FRUIT AUX POMMES

This recipe makes a delicious sweetmeat, using the otherwise wasted apple pulp from the Geranium Jelly (above). The *pâte de fruit* will be ready in a few days if left in an airing cupboard, but will take up to a fortnight if kept in a cool, dry place.

ALLOW:
500 g/1 lb granulated sugar for each 500 ml/pint of apple pulp.

In a preserving pan put the pulp and sugar. Heat gently until melted, then raise the heat and boil for about 15 minutes. Stir from time to time to avoid the pulp catching at the bottom of the pan. Beware of hot splatterings. When a little of the apple pulp sets when tested on a plate, it is ready. Pour into lightly oiled, shallow tins. Allow to dry, preferably in a warm, dry place. When the *pâte* has shrunk a little from the sides of the tins and the top is dry, invert onto a board and cut in squares. Roll each square in sugar, stick in a split almond if you like. Serve at the end of a meal with coffee or tisane.

JUNIPER JELLY

This jelly has an apple base, flavoured with woody-scented juniper berries. It makes a nice change from redcurrant jelly, served with game or pork. You can use windfall cooking apples like Bramleys.

FOR 2 POTS

1 kg/2 lb cooking apples
500 ml/1 pint water
60 g/2 oz juniper berries, lightly crushed

1 teaspoon coriander seeds, lightly crushed
preserving sugar

Chop the apples roughly with their skin and core. Put into an enamelled saucepan with the water and the crushed berries and seeds tied in a muslin bag. Simmer until soft, stirring from time to time. Then put the pulp in a jelly-bag and let it drain until no more juice drips. Measure the volume of juice and for each 500 ml/pint allow about 500 g/1 lb of sugar. Return the juice to the pan and stir in the sugar. Boil briskly until 1 drop put on a cool plate becomes sticky when pushed with a finger. Pour into clean, warmed jars and cover.

CRÉOLE JAM

One of my favourites. Because of its alcohol content it is definitely not for breakfast, but is excellent served at the end of a meal with fromage blanc (p. 16).

FOR 4–5 POTS

1 ½ kg/3 lb bananas	1 coffeespoonful powdered
1 kg/2 lb caster sugar	cinnamon
250 ml/½ pint water	125 ml/¼ pint rum
2 large lemons or 3 limes	

Peel the bananas, cut into slices and blanch in boiling water for 1 minute. Leave to drain. Prepare a syrup with the sugar and 250 ml/½ pint of water. Add the bananas and cook for 25 minutes. Meanwhile peel the lemons or limes, taking care to leave the pith on the fruit. Cut the zest into thin shreds (scissors are best for this) and blanch for 2 minutes. Drain. Squeeze the lemons or limes and add their juice to the bananas with the zest and cinnamon powder. Leave to thicken for 15 minutes more, stirring from time to time. Take off the heat, pour in the rum, mix well and put into jars.

COCONUT AND LEMON CURD

The creamed coconut which in this recipe replaces most of the butter, complements the savour of the lemon. It also makes this curd more economical.

FOR 2 POTS

2 very large lemons	60 g/2 oz creamed coconut
250 g/8 oz sugar cubes	3 eggs, lightly beaten
30 g/1 oz butter	

Rub the lemon skins with the sugar cubes to extract the scented essence. In the top of a double boiler, gently melt the butter and coconut. (The coconut is much slower to melt.) Then add the sugar cubes and the lemon juice, together with the strained eggs. Stir constantly until the curd thickens. Pour into the warmed jars, cover and label. Store in a cool place. It is delicious with banana bread (p.42).

DULCE DE LECHE

This is of South American origin and very sweet indeed. It should be served at tea time in the country on a rainy day. *Dulce de leche* takes a long time to cook, but if you can leave the pan on the top of an Aga for several hours it is not extravagant.

Put a large, unopened tin of sweetened condensed milk in a saucepan. Cover with water and bring to the boil. Reduce the heat and simmer for 2 hours checking the water level from time to time. Let it cool in the pan for 15 minutes, then take out, open, and transfer the caramel-coloured jam to a pot. Serve with toast.

DRINKS

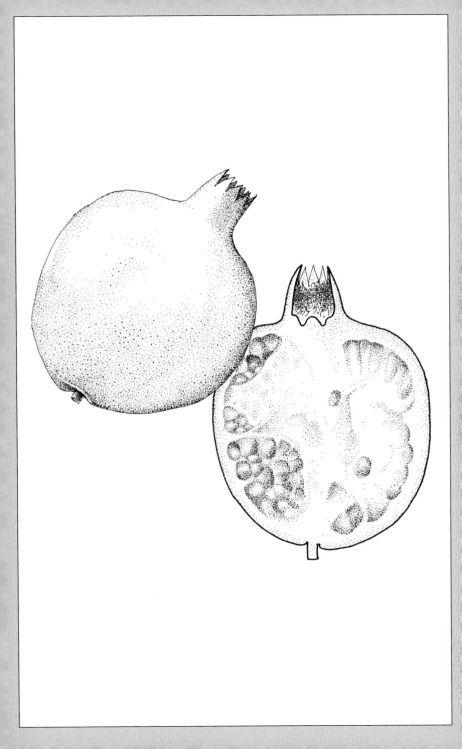

APHRODISIAC

This tisane is ironically called an aphrodisiac: it is in fact a reliable soporific. I make it often after our holidays in Provence. The hillsides around the house there are covered with wild thyme and rosemary. I bring back a large bunch of each, tied tight, which I place in a vase like a dried bouquet, clipping off the herbs as needed for cooking. In the right season, the concoction is made with the fresh, tiny, purplish-blue, fragrant flowers. The tisane should preferably be sweetened with lavender honey.

a large sprig of rosemary
a large sprig of thyme

about 500 ml/1 pint boiling water
honey

First warm a teapot with hot water and tip it out. Put the 2 sprigs inside and pour over the boiling water. Infuse for a few minutes and serve in delicate china cups, sweetened to taste with honey.

CAFÉ FLORENTINE

To enhance a hot cup of strong, fresh coffee add to the cup, before pouring in the coffee, just one drop of pure, bitter almond oil. Though I drink hot coffee unsweetened, I like it with a little sugar if I am adding almond oil. As a special treat, serve it with amaretti biscuits, these crisp Italian macaroons wrapped inside twists of paper of different colours.

FROTHY ICED COFFEE

I remember a few years ago, walking through the streets of New York, harassed by the August heat-wave. I went into the office building of a Colombian friend who happened to deal in coffee. As a public relations gesture, the ground floor had a bar where Colombian coffee, hot or iced, could be sampled free. To my surprise, there were very few people there. Young smiling students, working there to learn English, waited on you. I decided to try the iced coffee, not knowing what to expect, for under the same name I have been served drinks containing vanilla ice cream, milk or cream and even a kind of granita made with finely powdered coffee beans. A frothy concoction of a pale brown shade was put before me. I sipped a little of the creamy mixture. It was sheer bliss, truly refreshing, smooth, and hardly sweetened. I asked what the ingredient besides coffee was – cream, milk? I discovered that it was merely coffee, crushed ice and a very little sugar, whisked together at great speed for a few minutes in a liquidiser. I presume that the sugar, thus beaten with the other ingredients, helps make a froth.

The iced coffee should be made just before drinking, otherwise it starts to separate. It looks attractive served in tall glasses, with a drinking straw tucked in. It will quench your thirst and help you regain energy.

FOR 2

250 ml/½ pint very strong, fresh coffee, cooled	1 tablespoon caster sugar
	250 ml/½ pint crushed ice

Put all the ingredients in a liquidiser and blend until pale brown and frothy. Pour into 2 stemmed glasses. Serve at once with drinking straws.

CHILLED POMEGRANATE NECTAR

This is a truly refreshing drink to make when pomegranates are plentiful and inexpensive. It makes an unusual cocktail with vodka added to it, but I prefer the nectar without alcohol.

8 pomegranates, freshly squeezed like oranges juice of 1 lemon	about 4 tablespoons sugar crushed ice

Stir all the ingredients in a jug and chill. Serve in frosted glasses with a sprig of mint and perhaps more ice.

STORE CUPBOARD

Though not all the ingredients listed below are used for the recipes in this book, they are useful for giving a new or unusual flavour to standard dishes. Use your imagination to invent and experiment.

SPICES
Allspice
Cardamom, in the pod
Cinnamon, bark and ground
Cloves, whole and ground
Coriander seeds
Juniper berries
Lemon grass, ground
Mace, blades and ground
Mustard seeds
Nutmeg, whole
Paprika
Peppers
  Black peppercorns
  Cayenne pepper
  Green peppercorns, freeze-dried
  Red peppercorns, freeze-dried
  White peppercorns
Saffron stigmas
Star anise
Turmeric, ground
Vanilla pods

SAUCES AND FLAVOURINGS
Angostura bitters
Curry paste
Hellmann's mayonnaise
Liquid hickory smoke
Maggi sauce

Mustards
  Dijon mustard
  Meaux mustard with seeds
  Maille mustard with green herbs
Soy sauce
Tabasco sauce
Tomato paste
Worcestershire sauce

SWEET FLAVOURINGS
Almond essence, natural
Cinnamon flavour, natural
Orange-flower water
Rose-water
Vanilla essence, natural

GRAINS AND PULSES
Burghul, medium
Couscous, medium
Flageolets
Lentils, green
Polenta, medium
Rice
  Brown rice
  Piemontese rice
  Wild rice

BISCUITS
Bath Oliver biscuits
Charcoal biscuits

Pumpernickel
Siljans rye biscuits

OILS
Basil oil
Garlic oil
Peanut oil
Sesame oil
Sunflower oil
Virgin olive oil
Walnut oil

VINEGARS
Cider vinegar
Raspberry vinegar
Sherry vinegar
Tarragon vinegar

DRIED HERBS
Bay leaves
Chive
Dill weed
Oregano
Rosemary
Tarragon
Thyme

SEEDS
Aniseed
Caraway seeds
Fennel seeds
Sesame seeds

SALT
Celery salt
Coarse sea salt
Table sea salt

SUGAR
Coffee sugar crystals
Demerara sugar
Muscovado dark sugar
Muscovado light sugar
Vanilla caster sugar

SPIRITS
Calvados
Cognac
Cointreau
Crème de cacao
Coconut liqueur
Ginger wine
Pernod
Rum

FLOURS
Buckwheat flour
Chestnut flour
Chick-pea flour
Cornflour
Oatmeal, coarse
Rice flour
Rolled oats
Unbleached white flour
Wholemeal flour
Dried yeast

NUTS
Almonds
Coconut, desiccated
Hazelnuts
Pine nuts
Peanuts, roasted
Pistachio nuts
Walnuts

DRIED FRUITS
Apricots, Turkish and Hunza*
Bananas
Citron peel
Dates
Figs
Ginger, crystallised
Orange peel
Peaches
Pears
Prunes

TINNED FOODS
Campbell's clear consommé
Chick-peas
Corn kernels
Lychees
Red kidney beans
Smoked mussels
Smoked oysters
Tiny baby corns
Water chestnuts

PRESERVES
Chutneys
Honeys
Jams and preserves
Pickles

Hunza apricots: untreated wild
apricots from Afghanistan. They
are more perfumed and have a
milder taste than the common
apricots. The kernel inside the
stone is delicious too, and not
bitter. Soak in warm water for
a couple of hours, then use
sweetened, on their own, or
stoned as a filling for a tart.

TISANES
Camomile
Hibiscus flowers
Spearmint
Rose-hips

FLOWERS FOR COOKING
Elderflowers, dried
Marigolds, dried

CHINA TEAS
Jasmine
Earl Grey
Lapsang Souchong
Oolong
Rose

COCOA AND COFFEE
Dutch cocoa powder
Trablit pure coffee extract

IN THE REFRIGERATOR
Cheese rennet
Creamed coconut
Filo pastry (can also be frozen in
    plastic bags)
Ginger root, fresh
Horseradish, grated, in a jar
Vine leaves in brine

INDEX